BED and BREAKFAST: CALIFORNIA

ELK COVE INN

BED and BREAKFAST: CALIFORNIA

A Selective Guide

by Linda Kay Bristow

Illustrated by Linda Herman

CHRONICLE BOOKS   SAN FRANCISCO

LIBRARY OF CONGRESS CATALOGING IN
PUBLICATION DATA
Bristow, Linda Kay.
  Bed and breakfast, California.

  Includes index.
  1. Bed and breakfast accommodations —
California — Directories. I. Title.
TX907.B736 1985 674'.94724 85-3823
ISBN 0-87701-332-2 (pbk.)

BOOK AND COVER DESIGN: Linda Herman
CARTOGRAPHY: Terry Milne
COMPOSITION: Accent & Alphabet, Seattle
FRONT COVER: Courtesy of Hermitage House
                         Photography by Russel Abraham
BACK COVER: Courtesy of Red Castle Inn
                         Photography by Jeff Lapides

PHOTO CREDITS
Page 3, courtesy of The Spreckels Mansion;
page 5, Russell Abraham; page 11, courtesy
of the Bed and Breakfast Inn; page 21,
courtesy of The Red Victorian; page 27,
Patricia Bolfing; page 39, courtesy of Holly
Tree Inn; page 41, courtesy of Ten Inverness
Way; page 47, courtesy of Pygmalion House;
page 53, courtesy of Grape Leaf Inn; page 59,
Youngblood Photography, Healdsburg; page
65, Jim Beazley; page 67, courtesy of La
Residence Country Inn; page 71, Susan
Spann; page 83, courtesy of Chalet Bernensis;
page 85, courtesy of Chestelson House; page
105, courtesy of the Elk Cove Inn; page 111,
courtesy of Glendeven; page 113, courtesy of
the Headlands Inn; page 115, courtesy of the
Joshua Grindle Inn; page 139, courtesy of the
Carter House Inn; page 147, courtesy of the
Mayfield House; pages 177 and 187, Pat
Hathaway; page 203, courtesy of The
Parsonage.

10   9   8   7   6   5   4   3   2   1

Chronicle Books
One Hallidie Plaza
San Francisco
California 94102

Table of Contents

Preface

When I began researching inns for *Bed and Breakfast: California* I was looking for places that fit my preconceived notion of what a bed and breakfast should be: a home with four to six guest rooms, owner occupied, at a reasonable price, breakfast inclusive. It didn't take long to realize that looking for the "definition-perfect" bed and breakfast was like looking for a needle in a haystack. Inns come in all sizes, shapes, and price ranges. They vary greatly, due to factors such as locale, architectural style, and owner. And unlike their European counterparts, the American versions tend to offer an interesting alternative to the hotel/motel syndrome rather than an inexpensive night's lodging in someone's home.

In 1982 I was hard-pressed to find enough inns to fill a book. Today there are nearly four hundred bed and breakfasts in California, and I hear of new ones all the time. In the following pages you'll find a review of 101 such establishments in the state. Most are in areas of scenic or historic interest: the Wine Country, the Mendocino coast, the Gold Country, to name a few. Some are well known, others unknown. They are housed in buildings ranging in style from turn-of-the-century Queen Anne Victorians to former hunting lodges to newly built structures of concrete and glass. They may contain as few as one room to as many as twenty-one rooms. I have visited or stayed at almost all of them and have endeavored to give them a fair appraisal.

There is a certain etiquette involved with the bed and breakfast experience, and since forewarned is forearmed, here are some pointers to make you feel at home:

1. The basic modus operandi is the same as if you were staying at the home of a friend. Express appreciation for the offerings, be considerate, and don't treat the owner-innkeeper like a servant.

2. Don't hesitate to ask for what you want or need.

3. Clean up after yourself in a shared-bath situation.

4. Say goodbye when you check out, and return the key personally.

5. Follow house rules concerning check-out time, parking locations, payment arrangements, etc.

Some other points to remember: Rates are subject to change. (The rate structure I've used throughout the book can be interpreted as follows: inexpensive — under $50; moderate — $50 to $75; expensive — $75 plus.) Reservations are a must. (Though many inns book well in advance, last-minute cancellations do occur — don't hesitate to phone and ask.) A private bath is usually hard to come by. Don't expect a telephone, television, or room service. Smoking is discouraged, pets are unwelcome, and children are subject to house policy. Some inns require a two-day minimum stay, especially through weekend or holiday periods.

I enjoyed the inns, as I know you will, and I'd like to take this opportunity to extend my appreciation to the innkeepers throughout the state for putting me up as well as for putting up with me. A special thanks to the members of the Santa Barbara Innkeepers' Association for their many useful ideas and a taste of what the business is like from the innkeeper's side of the fence. Immeasurable gratitude to my dear friend and copy editor, Helga Wall.

SPRECKELS MANSION

SAN FRANCISCO

The PENINSULA

Archbishops Mansion
Bed and Breakfast Inn
Hermitage House
Inn on Castro
Mansion Hotel
Monte Cristo
Obrero Hotel
Red Victorian
Spreckels Mansion
Union Street Inn
Washington Square Inn

Oakland

San Francisco

80

101

280

92

1

Half Moon Bay

San Benito House

Mountain View

Sunnyvale

101

Sunnyside

280

85

Fairview Manor

Chateau Victorian
Cliff Crest Bed & Breakfast Inn

Spreckels Mansion

737 Buena Vista West
San Francisco, California 94117; (415) 861-3008

INNKEEPERS:	*Jonathan Shannon and Jeffrey Ross.*
ACCOMMODATIONS:	*Five rooms, four with private bath; queen-size beds.*
RESERVATIONS:	*Six weeks recommended.*
MINIMUM STAY:	*Two nights on weekends.*
DEPOSIT:	*First night's lodging.*
CREDIT CARDS:	*MC, VISA.*
RATES:	*Expensive.*
RESTRICTIONS:	*No children, pets, or cigar smoking.*

J onathan Shannon likes to think of the Spreckels Mansion as "a country inn in the city." And indeed he has a point. This elegant Victorian, built in 1887 for Richard Spreckels, sits high on a hill in a quiet neighborhood overlooking San Francisco's Buena Vista Park.

Of all the bed and breakfast inns I visited in San Francisco, this is one of my favorites. The atmosphere is comfortable, the rooms are spacious, the innkeepers are delightful, and there is plenty of parking (I mention this because in San Francisco parking space is a rare commodity).

Each room reflects the innkeepers' philosophy that "the room is as important a part of the traveler's experience as anything else." With the exception of the San Francisco suite, all the rooms are Victorian in feeling. Each is appointed with antiques, family treasures, and quality furniture. And each features an incredible view of the city. The San Francisco suite, which takes up the whole third story of the house, is decorated with contemporary furnishings and boasts a view of the city's skyline. The Sugar Baron suite is graced with tall fan windows, Corinthian columns, a pictorial-tile mantelpiece, and a canopied alcove that holds a queen-size bed. Its private bath is so enormous that you think you are walking into yet another suite. And what I wouldn't give for a soak in the freestanding tub in front of the fireplace just about now.

Breakfast at the Spreckels Mansion is light Continental: croissants, orange juice, and coffee or tea. In the evening guests (sometimes including United Nations ambassadors and Hollywood celebrities) mingle in the parlor to sip complimentary wine.

Nearby attractions include Haight Street shops and restaurants and Golden Gate Park. The inn is only fifteen minutes from downtown and the city's waterfront.

Archbishops Mansion

1000 Fulton Street
San Francisco, California 94117; (415) 563-7872

INNKEEPERS:	*Jonathan Shannon and Jeffrey Ross.*
ACCOMMODATIONS:	*Fifteen rooms, all with private bath; queen-size beds.*
RESERVATIONS:	*Three to four weeks recommended.*
MINIMUM STAY:	*Two nights on weekends.*
DEPOSIT:	*Two nights' lodging.*
CREDIT CARDS:	*AE, MC, VISA.*
RATES:	*Expensive.*
RESTRICTIONS:	*No pets.*

T hey've done it again, this irrepressible pair. And everyone's talking about it. (Bob and Sue Garmston, innkeepers of the Briggs House in Sacramento, spent their fifth wedding anniversary here and called it "a masterpiece"; in the guest ledger I spotted the names of other innkeepers looking for the ultimate getaway for themselves.) I could hardly complete my interview with the innkeepers, what with calls coming in from reporters and radio talk-show hosts. It's the Archbishops Mansion, San Francisco's newest bed and breakfast inn; one that renders European elegance in a style only Jonathan Shannon (impeccable taste with a touch of flamboyance) and Jeffrey Ross (exhaustive knowledge of architectural history and restoration) could achieve.

Built in 1904 to house the offices and residences of the archbishops of San Francisco, this Second Empire French building with its fifteen bedrooms and eighteen working fireplaces is one of the city's three largest homes — thirty thousand square feet in all. The interior follows the classical style of the French Renaissance (Beaux-Arts), with receiving rooms located on the first floor and bedrooms occupying the second and third floors. The parlor, the buffet between the outside world and the one within, is handsomely appointed with Oriental carpets, fine oil paintings, a mix of European, Victorian, and Oriental antiques, a floor-to-ceiling gold-leaf mirror, and vases of tiger lilies in bloom. (Take special note of the triple-vaulted ceiling, crystal chandelier, and massive carved-redwood fireplace.) A magnificent oval glass dome hovers above the stairwell leading to the guest rooms, which are named after romantic operas: La Bohème, Manon, Tosca, Carmen, Don Giovanni, Turandot, and Madame Butterfly.

Same-day laundry and dry cleaning service, room service (for snacks), and complimentary soft drinks are among the amenities seldom heard of at other inns. Champagne and wine are available for purchase; wine tastings are a tradition. For breakfast the inn serves what's reputed to be the city's best croissant, along with orange juice and coffee.

The Archbishops Mansion overlooks Alamo Square, one of the city's registered historic districts, which encompasses more Victorian architecture than any other neighborhood. (You may recognize the row of Victorians along Steiner Street from a well-known picture postcard.) Davies Symphony Hall, the Opera House, the Museum of Modern Art, and the Civic Center are just six blocks away. Eight blocks in the other direction is Golden Gate Park.

Hermitage House

2224 Sacramento Street
San Francisco, California 94115; (415) 921-5515

INNKEEPERS:	Dr. and Mrs. Frederick Binkley.
ACCOMMODATIONS:	Six guest rooms, all with private bath; twin, double, queen-, and king-size beds.
RESERVATIONS:	Three months recommended.
MINIMUM STAY:	Preference given to guests requesting five nights or more.
DEPOSIT:	First and last night's lodging.
CREDIT CARDS:	MC, VISA.
RATES:	Moderate to expensive.
RESTRICTIONS:	No children. No pets.

Marian Binkley told me that for the past several years she has enjoyed "restoring old buildings on a shoestring." But as I toured the Hermitage House with her, I was quickly convinced that this lovely home was restored on much more than a shoestring (to say nothing of many hours of hard work). In fact, I remembered the building from the mid-seventies when it housed a drug rehabilitation center, and I could hardly believe the transformation.

This four-story Greek Revival was originally built for Judge Charles Slack sometime between 1900 and 1903. The Binkleys purchased the house in 1978 with the intent of turning it into rental units. But its ten bedrooms, seven working fireplaces, and spacious common areas made the house a natural for a bed and breakfast inn.

Two flights of stairs lead to the main entrance of the all-redwood house. Inside, the entryway shows off the beautiful carved heart redwood detail of the period in the pillars, beams, and stairway scrolls. High ceilings mark the first two main stories, and intricate inlaid designs are worked into the edging of the hardwood floors in the living room. A small alcove to the right of the entry was once used as a chapel for weddings and christenings.

Another flight of stairs leads to the bedrooms, the most impressive of which are Judge Slack's Study with its redwood shakes, beamed ceiling, bookshelf-lined walls, massive king-size bed, and view of the city; and the Master Bedroom with a king-size bed, a cozy sitting area in front of a fireplace, and a footed tub in its private bath.

The other natural that makes Hermitage House such a success as a bed and breakfast inn is Marion Binkley. She not only shows genuine interest in her guests, but her philosophy that "a bed and breakfast inn should be small, cozy, and homelike with a single (and stable) guiding force behind it" shines through.

Early risers will appreciate the ample breakfast, which is served buffet style in the downstairs breakfast room from 7:30 A.M. on. The fare consists of freshly squeezed orange juice, a selection of rolls with butter and jam, an assortment of hot and cold cereals, fruit, coffee, tea, and hot chocolate.

Hermitage House is one of only a few inns that allow (and even encourage) guests to make use of the kitchen facilities, which are conveniently set up for cooking and serving meals. The refrigerator can be used to store groceries, and all the other essentials (pans, dishes, and utensils) are on hand. This, along with private phones available on request and laundry and dry cleaning services, makes the Hermitage House more than just an inn. In fact, major corporations refer their favorite clients and top executives to the Hermitage.

The inn is located in the city's Pacific Heights district. The No. 1 California bus (which goes to the heart of the financial district) stops across the street. The Fillmore and Union Street shopping areas are within walking distance, and Japantown is just a few blocks away.

Union Street Inn

2229 Union Street
San Francisco, California 94123; (415) 346-0424

INNKEEPER:	Helen Stewart.
ACCOMMODATIONS:	Five rooms, two with private bath; double, queen-, and king-size beds. Carriage House.
RESERVATIONS:	Six weeks recommended.
MINIMUM STAY:	Two nights on weekends.
DEPOSIT:	First and last night's lodging.
CREDIT CARDS:	AE, MC, VISA.
RATES:	Expensive.
RESTRICTIONS:	Children: Minimum age 12. No pets.

F or Helen Stewart, owning and operating a bed and breakfast inn is a third career. As a mother she raised five children, and she has also taught school. As an innkeeper she is a natural. Helen's appealing calmness is reflected in the decor and surroundings of her Union Street Inn.

This two-story house, an Edwardian built around the turn of the century, is slightly set back from the bustle of Union Street. A few steps lead to a small front porch that opens to the reception area and downstairs parlor. The parlor, where guests gather in the late morning and early evening, has a soft apricot velvet wall covering, a brick fireplace, bay windows, and glass doors that open out to a back deck and garden. The furnishings, rich in tone and texture, are contemporary with a mix of antiques; the most unusual pieces are a pair of iron and brass chairs, with leather backs and seats, that were made in Australia. A bowl of potpourri made from the flowers in the garden sits on one of the end tables.

There are five bedrooms; two have a private bath and the other three share two bathrooms. Although the rooms range in price from $75 to $105 per night, I found one to be just as nice as the next. Wildrose (one of the least expensive) has a persimmon-mauve decor and features a double brass bed, an abundance of healthy-looking green plants, and a garden view. The Golden Gate room, with a queen-size canopy bed in contrasting shades of midnight blue and mocha-cream, looks out to Union Street. To ease the "shared bath" situation there are sinks in every room, and bathrobes are provided.

The most recent addition is the Carriage House — a romantic hideaway with its own patio, garden, and Jacuzzi.

The morning I spent at the Union Street Inn I relaxed on the sun deck with a glass of orange juice, a steaming hot cup of coffee, and one of the most delicious croissants I've ever tasted. Helen told me that she and her staff "taste-tested" just about every croissant made in San Francisco until they finally settled on one made at a French bakery a few blocks away. Between the breakfast, the morning sun, and the gentle breeze that filled my senses with the fragrance of the many varieties of flowers in the garden, I found it difficult to leave.

Those who can manage to tear themselves away from this peaceful and visually pleasant environment will find some of the city's finest shops and restaurants just a short distance from the door. Fisherman's Wharf, Pier 39, the new symphony center, the Opera House, and downtown San Francisco are minutes away.

The Bed and Breakfast Inn

Four Charlton Court
San Francisco, California 94123; (415) 921-9784

INNKEEPERS:	*Robert and Marily Kavanaugh.*
ACCOMMODATIONS:	*Ten rooms, six with private bath; twin, double, queen-, and king-sized beds.*
RESERVATIONS:	*Two to three months recommended.*
MINIMUM STAY:	*None.*
DEPOSIT:	*First night's lodging.*
CREDIT CARDS:	*Not accepted.*
RATES:	*Moderate to expensive.*
RESTRICTIONS:	*Children: Minimum age 12. No pets.*

T he Bed and Breakfast Inn, opened in 1976, was the first b&b in San Francisco. Many have opened since, but this is still one of the most popular in the city, evidenced by comments like this one in the inn's guest book: "In my fifteen years of coming to San Francisco this was my favorite visit because of you."

At the time of the inn's opening, the owners, Robert and Marily Kavanaugh, didn't realize they had hit on an idea whose time had come. Having traveled extensively, they were anxious to open an inn patterned after those they had stayed at in Wales and Scotland. Bob's background in real estate and building and Marily's industriousness and flair for decorating led them to purchase and restore this one-hundred-year-old Victorian, which is located in a quiet cul-de-sac off fashionable Union Street that reminds one of a London mews.

Although today the Kavanaughs are assisted by a friendly staff of five, Marily explained that they did everything themselves for the first three years they were in business. I didn't find this hard to believe, as the afternoon I arrived I found her ironing table linens while Bob was busy with odd jobs in the garden.

It is apparent that the Kavanaughs take great pride

in what they do — and they do it well. On arrival, guests are greeted on a first-name basis and escorted to their room, where personal touches such as fresh flowers and fruit are evident.

Many of the rooms, such as the Mayfair, Covent Garden, and Kensington Gardens, are named after areas of London. Each room is unique in decor; antiques and family heirlooms are judiciously scattered throughout.

My favorite room is Celebration, one of the four available with a private bath. And what a bath — complete with a sunken double tub, a hand-painted Sherle Wagner pedestal basin, plush towels, and scented soaps and bath oil. The bedroom, papered with a blue and white Laura Ashley print, features a love seat and a queen-size bed. Another popular guest room (and one of the two that open to the garden) is the Willows, decorated in green and white print accented by white wicker furniture.

The Continental breakfast, served on Wedgwood china, includes fresh-squeezed orange juice, warm croissants, freshly ground coffee, and herbal tea. Evening sherry is complimentary, current magazines and good books are plentiful, and, unlike many other b&b inns, rooms with televisions and telephones are available.

The Bed and Breakfast Inn is located between Laguna and Buchanan in the heart of Union Street's sixteen blocks of boutiques, restaurants, and antique shops.

Inn on Castro

321 Castro Street
San Francisco, California 94114; (415) 861-0321

INNKEEPER:	*Joel Roman.*
ACCOMMODATIONS:	*Five rooms, all with private bath; dual twin and king-size beds.*
RESERVATIONS:	*Four to six weeks recommended.*
MINIMUM STAY:	*Two nights; three over holiday periods.*
DEPOSIT:	*Two nights' lodging.*
CREDIT CARDS:	*AE, MC, VISA.*
RATES:	*Moderate to expensive.*
RESTRICTIONS:	*No pets.*

The Inn on Castro, though housed in a 1910 Victorian (just up the hill from the intersection of Market and Castro streets), is strictly contemporary in interior design and furnishings. Although the mix of guests ranges from royalty to prim and proper elderly ladies, the inn caters primarily to a gay clientele.

The innkeeper (a native New Yorker) is Joel Roman, artist and interior designer. While attending L'Accademia delle Belle Arti in Bologna, Italy, Roman traveled through Europe, staying at bed and breakfast inns. He determined then to open one of his own in San Francisco when he returned to the United States. His inn, opened in 1980, now serves as his personal art gallery, with his works enhancing the guest rooms, hallways, and common areas.

The inn has five guest rooms, which all sport Italian names. The striking features of Il Camino (the Fireplace) are its ornate brass bed, wicker chairs and baskets, abundance of thriving green plants, multicolored umbrella ceiling, and bay windows with vertical blinds. La Serra (the Greenhouse) has a window that looks out to a greenhouse directly off the bedroom. A private phone is available on request. A pay phone as well as a wet bar (refrigerator, sink, and ice maker) are located in the central hallway that runs the length of the building.

Common areas (which serve as showplaces for Roman's glass collection) include the upstairs living room, a gathering place for stimulating conversation and informal cocktails in the late afternoon; and the dining room, where breakfast is served. Breakfast starts at 8:30 A.M. with a glass of fresh fruit juice (usually orange or grapefruit), heavenly croissants from Bakers of Paris (one of the city's well-known bakeries), butter and jams imported from London, and, of course, coffee and tea.

After breakfast you can wander around the Castro Street shops, see Mission Dolores, or take the bus to Haight Street or Golden Gate Park. Public transportation is plentiful.

Obrero Hotel

1208 Stockton Street
San Francisco, California 94133; (415) 989-3960

INNKEEPER:	*Bambi McDonald.*
ACCOMMODATIONS:	*Twelve rooms, all with shared baths; twin and double beds.*
RESERVATIONS:	*Two weeks recommended.*
MINIMUM STAY:	*Two nights.*
DEPOSIT:	*First and last night's lodging.*
CREDIT CARDS:	*Not accepted.*
RATES:	*Inexpensive.*
RESTRICTIONS:	*No pets. Quiet children are welcome.*

I would dub the Obrero Hotel the "no-frills bed and breakfast inn." But to use the words of the hotel's owner-innkeeper, Bambi McDonald, it is "a twelve-room (none of them perfect) European-style pension with an emphasis on cleanliness and value." And talk about value — this is certainly one of the least expensive places to stay in San Francisco (or anywhere, I might add), with prices ranging from $25 single to $45 triple occupancy.

But the Obrero is not for everyone, and it's not without its problems, as Bambi will be the first to admit. As a "for instance," the building's water heater only holds fifty gallons (I'll leave the rest to your imagination). But independent people interested in meeting similar types and in staying in the city at bargain prices find that the Obrero just fills the bill. A normal day at the hotel finds the gamut of visitors ranging from European students to bird-watchers from Bolinas, with a few filmmakers thrown in.

Because Ms. McDonald lived in Europe for several years and worked for friends who ran a pension in Amsterdam in exchange for room and board, she was not unfamiliar with the business. But striking out on her own in San Francisco wasn't as easy as she had imagined. It took three long, hard years to build up a reputation, and as she approaches her sixth year in business she still works seven days a week, twelve hours a day. In fact, she runs the whole operation with just one waitress, one maid, a strong dose of self-discipline, and a tight fist.

The hotel's twelve rooms share four baths, and the room furnishings are simple and sparse. Bambi describes a typical room as including "the best bed I could buy, a brass headboard, one chair, a dresser, a closet, and a sink with hot and cold running water."

Breakfast is served family style from 8:00 to 8:45 A.M., and it's enough to last through an entire day of sightseeing. A morning's sampling includes a four-minute egg, ham, cheese, an orange, hot sourdough bread, and tea and coffee — all included in the price of the room.

Family-style dinners featuring French Basque cuisine are served nightly. There are two entrées each night; sample fares include oxtail stew, cassoulet, Basque chicken, and shepherd's pie. Dinner comes with soup, salad, dessert, wine, and coffee — all for the bargain price of $9.50.

The hotel is conveniently located in the heart of San Francisco's Chinatown on the edge of North Beach, the Italian section of the city. Fisherman's Wharf and Union Square are just a stone's throw away.

The Monte Cristo

600 Presidio Avenue
San Francisco, California 94115; (415) 931-1875

INNKEEPER:	*Frances Allan.*
ACCOMMODATIONS:	*Eighteen rooms, fifteen with private bath; twin, double, and queen-size beds.*
RESERVATIONS:	*Three to four weeks recommended.*
MINIMUM STAY:	*None.*
DEPOSIT:	*First night's lodging.*
CREDIT CARDS:	*AE, MC, VISA.*
RATES:	*Moderate to expensive.*
RESTRICTIONS:	*No pets.*

A couple from Laramie, Wyoming, described their stay at the Monte Cristo, one of San Francisco's many delightful bed and breakfast inns, as "a page from a storybook romance." And it's certain that the Monte Cristo has had many pages of romance throughout its history, as it was originally built as a hotel in 1875 and was well known as a bordello at various times.

All that aside, surely today the Monte Cristo is at the height of its glory, thanks to the efforts of the current innkeeper, Frances Allan. Frances, a former nurse, a former Marinite, and a native of Winnipeg, Canada, is just the type you'd expect to find running an inn. She is a culturally sophisticated person who is anxious to please and is full of tidbits on current theater performances, gallery and museum exhibits, and the area's best restaurants. Because Frances lives on the premises, she feels that each individual is a guest in her home rather than just a paying client.

The Monte Cristo has been superbly restored. And once you enter your bedroom door, it can even be forgiven the long, narrow hallways that run the length of the building. With few exceptions, the rooms are spacious. All are quite comfortable. Furnishings are Early American and English antiques, and each room has a large silk flower arrangement color-keyed to the wallpaper. The rooms have various names and themes: the Violet Room, the Wicker Room, and, my favorite, the English Four-Poster Room, which is done in shades of blues, mauves, and beige.

The Chinese Wedding Bed Room has an elaborate and inviting teak bed with a down comforter. If you've never heard of a Chinese wedding bed, don't feel bad. Neither had I. A wedding gift to a bride from her parents, the wedding bed is handed down in the bride's family through the years, eventually becoming an heirloom. The wealthier the family, the more elaborate the bed. And from the looks of this one the family must have been the equivalent of America's Rockefellers. Chinese accents fill the rest of the room, and silk robes are provided for your use after a dip in the sunken tiled tub.

The Monte Cristo is one of the few inns in the city that serve a full breakfast. Everything is home baked. The orange juice is freshly squeezed. The coffee cake comes straight from the oven. I left asking for the pancake recipe (what's so special about pancakes? — wait until you've tried these).

The Monte Cristo is located at the corner of Pine and Presidio, just a short walk from the Sacramento Street shops and restaurants. Major bus lines take you to Golden Gate Park, Fisherman's Wharf, or downtown in about fifteen minutes.

The Mansion Hotel

2220 Sacramento Street
San Francisco, California 94115; (415) 929-9444

INNKEEPER:	*Robert Pritikin.*
ACCOMMODATIONS:	*Eighteen rooms, all with private bath; twin, double, and queen-size beds.*
RESERVATIONS:	*Two weeks recommended.*
MINIMUM STAY:	*None.*
DEPOSIT:	*First night's lodging.*
CREDIT CARDS:	*AE, MC, VISA.*
RATES:	*Expensive.*
RESTRICTIONS:	*No pets.*

Robert Pritikin's Mansion Hotel is one of those places I run into every once in a while that straddles the thin line dividing an inn from a small hotel. But there are certain features that move me to include it here. First of all, it's housed in a grand, twin-turreted Queen Anne Victorian that was built by Utah State Senator Richard Chambers in 1887. Secondly, the innkeeper's colorful personality, wit, and varied background make for lively conversation. And finally, there is an ample breakfast served in-room each morning.

The hotel is billed as "being in the middle of everything — yet a million miles away." "Everything" includes the not-too-distant downtown, Fisherman's Wharf, and North Beach areas. The "million miles away" is actually just a step away from the front porch to the grand foyer, with its gigantic crystal chandelier and a mural depicting the romantic characters who inhabited the Mansion nearly a century ago.

To the right of the foyer is the Music Room, the setting for nightly classical concerts and weekend magic shows. The innkeeper ("America's foremost classical saw player") is your master of ceremonies. The piano here is said to have belonged to Claudia Chambers, the Mansion's legendary haunt whose invisible fingers play classical requests. (Claudia's bad manners are attributed as the cause of a host of the hotel's problems and troubles. The staff snickers at the story of the night she unhinged a door that fell on the head of a guest who was being difficult.)

Another room worth noting is the Billiard Room. Beside the antique billiard table you'll find a stained-glass nickelodeon-player piano pumping out the tunes of John Philip Sousa and Scott Joplin. A collection of beaded Victorian purses is displayed on the wall above an outsized "dollhouse" that was the original set from Edward Albee's New York Broadway production of *Tiny Alice*. The glass-fronted armoires hold memorabilia.

Guest rooms occupy the second and third floors of the building. A brass plaque on the door of each room identifies the historic personage to whom the room is dedicated, and the walls of the room are alive with murals describing the legend of that person's life. Your room *may* have a marble fireplace, or a private terrace, or a ceiling that slants to the floor, but I can guarantee that it will have a painting of a pig. Though they seem to add to the fun, the paintings are not always appreciated. Guests frequently take them down and put them out in the hallway. In one of the rooms I toured with Pritikin the painting was not only down, it was turned to the wall.

Breakfast anyone? How does a French croissant, a wineglass full of fresh orange juice with a strawberry on the side, a hard-cooked "Easter" egg (found under the teacup), and freshly ground coffee sound?

Tennis? LaFayette Park is just a block away. Sauna? There's one in-house. Afternoon sherry? It's complimentary. Dinner? The hotel has an intimate dining room that features entrées fit for royalty. There's Double Breast of Duckling Nicole, the Czar's Pasta, and Suprême of Chicken Luxembourg (a dish the late Grand Duchess would have given her tiara for, says Master Chef David Coyle). Last but not least are the front and back gardens displaying a collection of Beniamino Bufano sculptures, the most prominent of which are two towering bronze figures of Saint Francis of Assisi, the patron saint of San Francisco.

The Red Victorian

1665 Haight Street
San Francisco, California 94117; (415) 864-1978

INNKEEPER:	*Sami Sunchild.*
ACCOMMODATIONS:	*Fifteen rooms, three with private bath; twin, double, queen-, and king-size beds.*
RESERVATIONS:	*Two weeks recommended.*
MINIMUM STAY:	*None.*
DEPOSIT:	*In full.*
CREDIT CARDS:	*MC, VISA.*
RATES:	*Inexpensive to moderate.*
RESTRICTIONS:	*No children. Pets by arrangement.*

Sami Sunchild is the artist-in-residence innkeeper; the Red Victorian is the grandest of all her works. This colorful bed and breakfast, located in the heart of San Francisco's ever-evolving Haight-Ashbury district, is a favorite of creative types and "new age" thinkers. Psychologists and architects, futurists and poets come here from as near as a block away to as far as New Zealand and the Orient.

This turn-of-the-century building was originally constructed as a resort hotel in the country. Today it is hard to believe that this area was ever "in the country." The hotel faded into a home for alcoholics and then in the 1960s it was invaded by hippies.

Sami purchased the property in 1977 and began single-handedly restoring the place to its original splendor. Today Sami believes that part of what makes the Red Victorian what it is is what it's not. It's not downtown. It's not in a frequented tourist area. And it's not for those who want to get away from it all or to just be alone. It is, however, conveniently located near Golden Gate Park and is on major bus lines to all parts of the city.

The inn's "pink parlor," with its red carpet, pink walls, and lace curtains with red velvet valances, is the setting for lively discussions and occasional seminars where locals and guests meet, exchange ideas, and make friends. There's a meditation room that, in Sami's words, "is so quiet you can hear the quiet." And Sami's "Lines of Thought" art gallery of calligraphic paintings dominates the second- and third-floor corridors.

The guest rooms (located off the long, narrow hallways that run the length of the building) are moderately priced. The least expensive is the Green Room, which overlooks Haight Street. The best room in the house is the Peacock Suite, which features an electric fireplace, a crystal chandelier, and a king-size bed. The rooms are all simply furnished. Handmade quilts, Haight Street memorabilia, and old photographs of the hotel accent each room.

A light Continental breakfast of croissants, coffee, tea, and orange juice is served from 8:00 A.M. to noon in the pink parlor.

The Washington Square Inn

1660 Stockton Street
San Francisco, California 94133; (415) 981-4220

INNKEEPERS:	*Nan and Norm Rosenblatt.*
ACCOMMODATIONS:	*Fifteen rooms, ten with private bath; twin, double, queen- and king-size beds.*
RESERVATIONS:	*Six to eight weeks recommended.*
MINIMUM STAY:	*None.*
DEPOSIT:	*First night's lodging.*
CREDIT CARDS:	*AE, MC, VISA.*
RATES:	*Moderate to expensive.*
RESTRICTIONS:	*Children discouraged. No pets.*

San Francisco's Nan and Norm Rosenblatt "got the bug" for a bed and breakfast inn of their own while traveling through Europe and staying at little inns along the way. Nan is an interior designer, Norm a financial wizard. Together they turned two dilapidated buildings that sat back to back into one fantastic inn: the Washington Square Inn.

A stay at the inn is so pleasant that it's tempting to stay in, especially if you have one of the three rooms that overlook the square. Although the rooms are individually decorated, a "European country" theme prevails. Furnishings are a well-balanced mix of antique and contemporary. The beds are all modern, but some have fabric canopies that blend with the soft floral-patterned drapes and bedspreads. Most rooms have a private bath and all have a telephone. Televisions are available on request. As in most of the other inns in this book, there are fresh flowers in every room.

Complimentary breakfast-in-bed runs to flaky croissants, freshly squeezed orange juice, coffee (Italian, of course), and herb tea. Or if you prefer to meet and mingle with the other guests, you can enjoy breakfast at the formal dining table in the reception lobby.

Though it may be tempting, don't linger over breakfast too long. Washington Square is in the heart of the city's colorful Italian district, which offers plenty to see and do. This area, called North Beach, is a favorite of locals and visitors alike for its specialty shops, bakeries, cafés, and nightclubs, all within a few blocks' radius.

And if that's not enough, the inn's concierge can arrange a car, theater tickets, a tour of the city, a picnic, or even a stenographer if you've come here to get down to business (heaven forbid). (Because the inn is midway between Fisherman's Wharf and the financial district, it appeals to tourists and business people alike.)

Tea, homemade shortbread, and cucumber sand-wiches are a complimentary afternoon affair.

Sunnyside

435 East McKinley Avenue
Sunnyvale, California 94086; (408) 736-3794

INNKEEPERS:	*Byrd and Phyllis Helligas.*
ACCOMMODATIONS:	*Two units, each with private bath; one double and one queen-size bed.*
RESERVATIONS:	*Two weeks recommended.*
MINIMUM STAY:	*None.*
DEPOSIT:	*First night's lodging.*
CREDIT CARDS:	*Not accepted.*
RATES:	*Inexpensive.*
RESTRICTIONS:	*No children. No pets.*

Byrd Helligas has worn a number of hats in his time. He was a Unitarian clergyman for thirteen years, he drove a delivery wagon, he once ran a political campaign, and he's worked in the food processing and tobacco industries. But the hat he wears now, and perhaps the hat he wears best, is that of innkeeper. Byrd is one of those people who can fascinate and entertain you at the same time with a million and one stories about a million and one things. And at Sunnyside, his "urban inn," there are at least that many things to talk about.

The inn, housed in a former potato chip factory, is a virtual museum of old and new junk that Helligas has rescued from the indifference of friends, city dumps, and other undisclosed sources. A turn-of-the-century, gas-fired candy cooker has been turned into a table. Discarded circuit boards from the Peninsula's thriving electronic firms cover the walls of one of the bathrooms. A soda ash firecart (of the type that was used to put out fires after San Francisco's 1906 quake) serves as a planter. The automatic stapler that was used to seal the factory's potato chip bags now sits as a piece of unusual sculpture on the front lawn.

There are two units, each with a private bath with an old-fashioned bathtub and shower, a television, and a telephone. The Reznor Room (named after the large industrial heater situated here) holds a queen-size bed (with an extra-firm mattress) built on an old Sears Roebuck display case. A down comforter "between the sheets" covers the bed. The room adjoins an atrium. The other unit, the Cottage, undoubtedly takes its name from the cottagelike feeling supplied by the beamed ceiling. It has a self-contained kitchen complete with pots and pans, dishes, and utensils. There's a double bed and an 1840s walnut and marble step dresser the Helligases call "the obscene queen."

Breakfast seems to be subject to the whims of the cook, but you have your choice of either a Continental or a full country breakfast whenever you'd like it within a reasonable time range. Mine consisted of a three-egg omelette, a banana, French bread with cream cheese and jam, coffee, and a glass of wine (well, I did get a rather late start).

Sunnyside is located within easy access of the major freeways (101 and 280). It's a twenty-minute drive from San Jose and about an hour from San Francisco. Sunnyvale's downtown shopping area is a short walk away.

San Benito House

356 Main Street
Half Moon Bay, California 94019; (415) 726-3425

INNKEEPER:	Carol Mickelsen.
ACCOMMODATIONS:	Twelve rooms, nine with private bath; double beds (one room with twin beds).
RESERVATIONS:	Three weeks recommended.
MINIMUM STAY:	None.
DEPOSIT:	First night's lodging.
CREDIT CARDS:	AE,MC,VISA.
RATES:	Inexpensive to moderate.
RESTRICTIONS:	No pets.

I can't wait to get back to San Benito House. This two-story, light-blue building on a corner of Half Moon Bay's Main Street offers a romantic bed and breakfast getaway just thirty-five miles south of San Francisco. Carol Mickelsen, part owner and chef-in-residence, oversees the whole operation, which consists of twelve guest rooms on the second floor, a downstairs restaurant that serves classic country cuisine, a Western-style saloon with "local color," and a garden deli-café.

The inn was originally built by Estanislaus Zabella at the turn of the century and was known as the Mosconi Hotel. In the 1930s it changed ownership and was renamed Domenic's. Mickelsen and partners (one of whom is husband Ron, owner of the Half Moon Bay Nursery) purchased the hostelry in 1976 and began a "three-phase" restoration project. The final phase (just completed at the time of my visit) entailed the careful restoration of each guest room to include fixtures and furnishings of the period.

The rooms are small but cozy. The one I called home was painted a forest green accented with white trim. There was a white iron bed with a fluffy comforter and an antique dresser with a huge bouquet of daisies in a wicker basket. (It helps to have a husband in the flower business.) Old photographs of the hotel and Half Moon

Bay scenes added a touch of interest, and a profusion of red geraniums in the flower box just outside the window added a splash of color. An upstairs deck provided a place to sit and look out over the ocean, and the sauna (the only modern concession in the whole place) was heavenly.

The evening started off with complimentary drinks in the saloon (weekends only), followed by a superb dinner of *fettuccine* with fresh *pesto,* a garden salad, and rack of lamb ($14.95). As if that wasn't enough, I couldn't resist one of the French pastries that San Benito House is so famous for, Le Montmorency, a very rich chocolate cake with apricots.

Even though I was still feeling slightly full from dinner the night before, I came down for breakfast. And I have to admit that I'm glad I did. There was a strong cup of Graffeo coffee, "fresh from the oven" whole-wheat bread with sweet butter and marmalade, a soft-boiled egg, and fresh fruit. Though breakfast is usually served in the dining room, it can be had out in the garden, or taken on a tray to the room for a leisurely breakfast in bed.

Half Moon Bay's Pacific Ocean setting offers uncrowded beaches and an outstanding tide pool area. There are hiking trails through a nearby redwood forest and several local wineries for touring. Whale watching, fishing, horseback riding, and bicycling are popular area activities.

Fairview Manor

245 Fairview Avenue
Ben Lomond, California 95005; (408) 336-3355

INNKEEPERS:	*John and Jackie Sullivan.*
ACCOMMODATIONS:	*Five rooms, three with private bath; double, queen-, and king-size beds.*
RESERVATIONS:	*Two to three weeks recommended.*
MINIMUM STAY:	*None.*
DEPOSIT:	*First night's lodging.*
CREDIT CARDS:	*MC, VISA.*
RATES:	*Moderate.*
RESTRICTIONS:	*No children under fourteen. No pets.*

I t was a quiet evening. We curled up on the sofa in front of a crackling wood fire, sipped champagne, and read. Neither of us spoke. To do so would have shattered the stillness. It was a time of solitude in togetherness. The misty fog that blanketed the Manor, the gentle ripple of the San Lorenzo River, and the lush greenery of the redwood forest just beyond the double French doors soothed body and soul.

We didn't see much of Jackie Sullivan; she made her well-timed entrances and exits to the rhythm of the daily routine in the life of an innkeeper — greeting her guests and showing them their room, setting out wine, cheese, and hors d'oeuvres at 5 o'clock, and not appearing again until breakfast the next morning. Her final curtain is check-out time.

Our late and leisurely breakfast consisted of freshly squeezed orange juice, a round of fresh pineapple artistically topped with melon balls and a sprig of fresh mint, a tray of warm pineapple muffins and blueberry coffee cake, a soft-boiled egg, and coffee. An hour or two of local antiqueing and a delightful afternoon aboard a vintage steam train rolling over narrow gauge rails at Roaring Camp in Felton followed.

We attempted to apologize for our tardiness at breakfast, but Jackie would have none of it. She told us that she used to serve breakfast at nine sharp, but felt that was a terrible hour to get people up, and one that missed the point of a vacation or weekend away entirely.

In an exchange of pleasantries with a honeymoon couple from southern California we discovered how many of this secluded retreat's patrons hear about the Manor — by glowing reports brought home from family and friends.

I suppose I should mention the fact that this was once the site of the famous Ben Lomond Hotel, point out the architectural style (Craftsman's bungalow, popular in the twenties), describe the furnishings (a mix of comfortable contemporary with French and English antiques scattered judiciously about) and mention artifacts on display from the Sullivans' world travels, or talk about the price of the room ($50–$65). But it all seems secondary to the total relaxation achieved here.

Chateau Victorian

118 First Street
Santa Cruz, California 95060; (408) 458-9458

INNKEEPER:	*Franz Benjamin.*
ACCOMMODATIONS:	*Seven rooms, all with private bath; queen-size beds.*
RESERVATIONS:	*Three to five weeks for summer weekends; two weeks off-season.*
MINIMUM STAY:	*None.*
DEPOSIT:	*First night's lodging.*
CREDIT CARDS:	*AE, MC, VISA.*
RATES:	*Moderate to expensive.*
RESTRICTIONS:	*No children. No pets.*

E ach year thousands of tourists flock to the beach at Santa Cruz. If you're one of them, and one who might enjoy a taste of gracious living at the same time, you'll be delighted to know about Chateau Victorian.

You won't have any problem spotting Chateau Victorian once you're in the neighborhood — which is crowded with motels and eateries and is just a block from the beach — it's painted bright orange (pumpkin, to be exact) with brown and white trim. A quaint Pennsylvania Dutch "Welcome" sign hangs in the front window.

One of the main attractions here is innkeeper Franz Benjamin, an easy-going, personable sort who fits right in with the beach's laid-back atmosphere. Of him a guest book entry raves: "You have elevated the business of innkeeping to an art form of which we are among the contented and appreciative beneficiaries."

Guest rooms have two things in common: queen-size beds and private baths. Some have fireplaces, one has an ocean view; antiques, brass beds, and window seats are much in evidence. The Patio Room (so named for its private entrance off the back patio) is decorated in a mauve and white Laura Ashley print and furnished with a white iron and brass bed, an armoire, and a wicker basket filled with ivy. Balloon shades cover the windows, and the original Victorian-era fireplace adds warmth on a cool summer's eve. Quite lovely.

The room I occupied, Natural Bridges, was warm and intimate with its delicately patterned beige and brown wallpaper, contrasting dark-wood ceiling beams, shuttered windows, iron and brass bed, and French armoire. And ooh-la-la — as the sun set, the lights were turned down, and the fireplace lit, I couldn't envision a more romantic hideaway.

"It's a wonderful life, this innkeeping life." Franz remarked as he poured my first cup of coffee of the morning. "Ninety-nine point nine percent of the people who walk through that front door are happy and looking for a good time." A second cup of coffee (an aromatic Viennese roast) was accompanied with freshly baked croissants with whipped unsalted butter, cream cheese, and orange marmalade. A platter of fresh fruit (papaya, melon, strawberries, blackberries, and bananas) was also part of this help-yourself buffet breakfast, scheduled from 9:00 to 10:30. I partook in the dining room, but Franz was equally agreeable to guests taking their breakfast to the patio or out to the front deck.

Locally produced Felton Empire and Bargetto wines, as well as cheese and crackers, were set out from 5:00 to 7:00 P.M. A nightcap of cognac was offered.

Besides the beach, the world-famous Santa Cruz Beach Boardwalk amusement park draws visitors from far and near. An interesting sidelight: more than twenty-five million people have ridden the boardwalk's Giant Dipper roller coaster, recognized as one of the ten best in the world. The city's annual events include a clam chowder cookoff in late February, a tug of war and volleyball tournament in May, the Miss California Pageant in June, and a wharf-to-wharf (Santa Cruz to Capitola) footrace in July.

Cliff Crest Bed & Breakfast In

407 Cliff Street
Santa Cruz, California 95060; (408) 427-2609

INNKEEPER:	*Cheryl McEnery.*
ACCOMMODATIONS:	*Five rooms, all with private bath; double and queen-size beds.*
RESERVATIONS:	*One month for weekends during the summer.*
MINIMUM STAY:	*None.*
DEPOSIT:	*First night's lodging.*
CREDIT CARDS:	*AE, MC, VISA.*
RATES:	*Moderate to expensive.*
RESTRICTIONS:	*No children. No pets.*

J ust up the hill from Chateau Victorian is Cliff Crest, a bed and breakfast inn that offers a quieter location from which to enjoy Santa Cruz's sandy beaches, fishing pier, and nostalgia-filled boardwalk. But Cliff Crest is a local historical landmark as well. It's the former residence of William Jeter, lieutenant governor of California (1890) and one-time mayor of Santa Cruz.

The home's five guest rooms are graced with antiques and fresh flowers. The Plum Room, a large fireplace room on the main floor, features an Eastlake Victorian queen-size bed, an armoire, hardwood floors with plum carpeting, and a garden view. A cozy upstairs hideaway is the Apricot Room, with its white antique double bed. The Grey Room (shades of soft blue and pale grey) offers a French queen-size bed and a tiled shower for two. The Rose Room, a sunny upstairs room with views of Monterey Bay and the Santa Cruz Mountains, has a sitting area and an adjacent bath with a Victorian claw-foot tub. The Pineapple Room, named for its four-poster bed with pineapples carved on the posts, harbors an 1887 stained-glass window.

Innkeeper Cheryl McEnery describes herself as "a person who likes to dote on others." And it's evident that she has gone out of her way to provide her guests with the comforts of a "home away from home": a lazy hammock between the trees, an umbrella table and chaise longue on the terrace, stimulating games (Trivial Pursuit, backgammon), and subscriptions to three daily newspapers (the *San Francisco Chronicle,* the *San Jose Mercury News,* and the *Santa Cruz Sentinel*).

Cheryl serves an inviting Continental breakfast (freshly squeezed orange juice, fresh fruits in season, French pastries, coffee, tea, and hot chocolate) to the room. If preferred, it can be enjoyed in the dining room, on the terrace, or in the solarium, with its picture windows looking out to the beautifully landscaped gardens designed by Mr. Jeter's friend, John McLaren, the landscape architect of Golden Gate Park.

THE PELICAN INN

MARIN COUNTY

SONOMA COUNTY

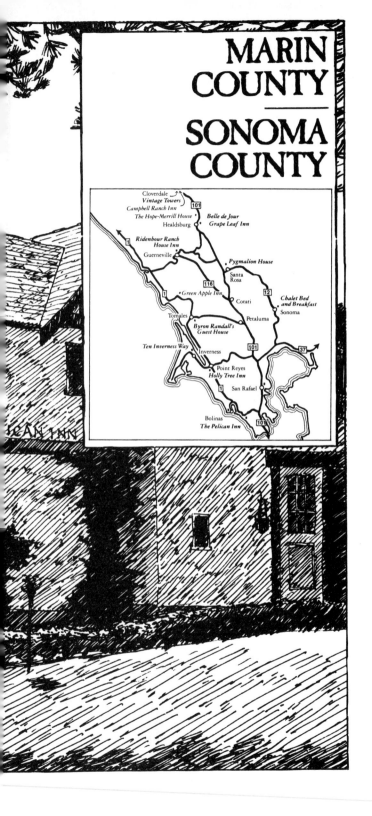

Cloverdale
Vintage Towers
Campbell Ranch Inn
The Hope-Merrill House
Healdsburg
Belle de Jour
Grape Leaf Inn

Ridenhour Ranch House Inn
Guerneville

Pygmalion House
Santa Rosa

Green Apple Inn
Cotati

Chalet Bed and Breakfast
Sonoma

Petaluma

Tomales
Byron Randall's Guest House

Ten Inverness Way
Inverness

Point Reyes
Holly Tree Inn
San Rafael

Bolinas
The Pelican Inn

ICAN INN

The Pelican Inn

10 Pacific Way
Muir Beach, California 94965; (415) 383-6000

INNKEEPERS:	*Charles and Brenda Felix.*
ACCOMMODATIONS:	*Six rooms, all with private bath; queen-size beds.*
RESERVATIONS:	*Six months recommended.*
MINIMUM STAY:	*None.*
DEPOSIT:	*In full.*
CREDIT CARDS:	*MC, VISA.*
RATES:	*Expensive.*
RESTRICTIONS:	*No pets.*

For bed and breakfast in the spirit of sixteenth-century England's west country, plan to stay at the Pelican Inn. The Pelican is located at Muir Beach, scarcely twenty minutes from the Golden Gate Bridge.

According to the innkeeper, Charles Felix, it was here on the Marin Coast that Sir Francis Drake beached his *Pelican* (the ship was renamed the *Golden Hinde* in mid-voyage) some four hundred years ago to claim California for Queen Elizabeth I and her descendants. Felix is not only a history buff, he's a fourth-generation publican of hearty British stock as well. In fact, he brought most of the Pelican Inn's furnishings and many of its superstitions from the family pub in Surrey.

The inn is a weathered-looking English Tudor-style farmhouse that sits nestled between the ocean and the redwoods of the Golden Gate National Recreation Area. The main floor of the building houses a traditional English pub and a public dining room. Pub grub includes meat pies, Scotch eggs, bangers, salads, home-baked bread, and desserts. The bar, with its low beams, dart board and good fellowship, is well stocked with imported brew (Bass, Watney, and John Courage on tap), wine, port, and sherry.

Overnight accommodations are located on the second floor. The rooms, with their low doorjambs and leaded windows, are graced with English antiques, heavily draped half-tester (canopy) beds, and Oriental rugs that cover the hardwood floors. Each room has a private bath. (Incidentally, the stone that hangs by a red silken thread over the bed is to insure that if conception occurs here the child will be born without rickets. "It's worked so far as I know," says Felix with a grin and a twinkle in his eye.)

Renaissance music, burning candles, and a roaring fire in the great inglenook set the tone for the proper English breakfast of bangers, bacon and eggs (any style), broiled tomatoes, toast with Scotch marmalade, orange juice, coffee, and tea. The dashing white-haired Felix can be found mingling among the guests, chatting about topics ranging from his San Francisco advertising business to moustache wax.

A stay of any length is like an ongoing tea party. (And speaking of tea, Darjeeling tea with biscuits and "all things nice" is served by the fire in the afternoon.) You never know what's going to happen next. There are Shakespearean excerpts, Elizabethan feasts, and English country dances on the front lawn.

Cricket, anyone?

Holly Tree Inn

Location: *3 Silverhills Road*
Inverness Park, California
Mailing address: *P.O. Box 642*
Point Reyes Station, CA 94956; (415) 663-1554

INNKEEPERS:	*Diane and Tom Balogh.*
ACCOMMODATIONS:	*Four rooms, two with private bath; double, queen-, and king-size beds.*
RESERVATIONS:	*Four weeks recommended.*
MINIMUM STAY:	*Two nights on weekends.*
DEPOSIT:	*In full.*
CREDIT CARDS:	*MC, VISA.*
RATES:	*Moderate.*
RESTRICTIONS:	*No pets.*

D iane Balogh relates a story about the afternoon a young couple rode up on horses to inquire about a room for the night. But this was nothing unusual as the Baloghs' inn — the Holly Tree Inn — is located just a mile or so from Point Reyes National Seashore, which offers a variety of outdoor activities, among them hiking, fishing, boating, bird-watching, beachcombing, whale watching, and, of course, horseback riding.

This comfortable and spacious two-story home reminiscent of a hunting lodge turned inn was built by a Swede in the late 1930s. The Baloghs, who had set their hearts on an inn of their own after staying at one in Maine in 1975, found the nineteen-acre estate on their first trip out with a realtor. They concluded the deal within a matter of days, moved in, and rented the downstairs as an apartment while the second-story conversion was taking shape. Opening day was July 14, 1979.

Central to the inn is the light, airy living room with its huge brick fireplace and overstuffed sofas uphol-stered in provincial prints. This is a wonderful place for conversation, a complimentary glass of wine in the after-noon, or a daydream or two.

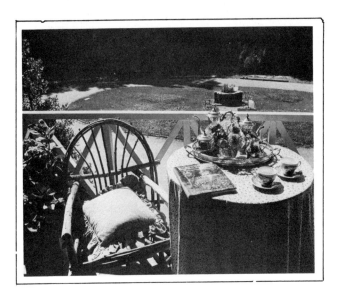

The living room opens up to the dining area, which also features a fireplace and a cozy setting for the 9:30 A.M. buffet-style breakfast. One morning it might include pancakes and sausage with fresh fruit, coffee, tea, and orange juice. The next you might get a sampling of Diane's quiche, or an omelette with homemade poppy seed bread.

There are only four guest rooms — the Laurel Room, the Holly Room, the Ivy Room, and the most recent addition, Mary's Garden — and I couldn't decide which I liked best. The Laurel Room is the most private as well as the largest. It is decorated in shades of pale blue and white, has a comfortable sitting area, and a king-size bed. The lace-edged sheets and white ruffled curtains set the mood in the Ivy Room, with its view of the flowery hillside and ivied latticework just outside the cottage windows. The Holly Room overlooks the front lawn with its flower-covered wishing well. Country antiques and peace and quiet are features the rooms have in common. the rooms have in common.

Unlike many other inns, the Holly Tree welcomes children. In fact the Baloghs have two very well-behaved children of their own.

Ten Inverness Way

10 Inverness Way
Inverness, California 94937; (415) 669-1648

INNKEEPERS:	Mary Davies and Stephen Kimball.
ACCOMMODATIONS:	Five rooms, all with shared bath; twin and double beds.
RESERVATIONS:	Four to six weeks recommended.
MINIMUM STAY:	Two nights on weekends.
DEPOSIT:	In full.
CREDIT CARDS:	Not accepted.
RATES:	Moderate.
RESTRICTIONS:	No pets.

T en Inverness Way is a five-bedroom, two-bath guest house that was built in 1904. The living room still has its original Douglas fir paneling and massive stone fireplace, and the guest rooms that were once family bedrooms retain that character. The entire house is furnished with what the proprietors call "comfortable antiques"; the rooms are filled with fresh flowers (daisies, fuchsias, carnations, and poppies, to name just a few) from the garden that surrounds the house.

Stephen Kimball (a building designer and contractor) and Mary Davies (a former Sacramento legislative director) are partners in the venture. Stephen backs the inn with money and muscle and Mary lends what can only be described as "the woman's touch": a feel for comfort, a flair for decorating, and a green thumb when it comes to gardening. Together, they've made Ten Inverness Way a "home away from home."

The living room is a great place to curl up with your favorite book. If you didn't bring one along you can choose from the wide selection that fills the bookshelf. The books (subjects range from religion to the arts, psychology to the classics) reflect the broad range of interests of the innkeepers. The player piano provides the evening's entertainment, and complimentary sherry can be enjoyed by the fire.

The bedrooms, all on the second floor, feature antique furniture, handmade rugs, and patchwork quilts. The most popular room in the house is at the top of the stairs. It's also the largest and the sunniest room; its four multipaned windows overlook the front garden.

There's a full American-style breakfast to start the day off right. Banana pancakes, quiche, and cheese-scrambled eggs are the specialties. Egg-based dishes might be complemented by homemade bread one morning or a freshly baked coffee cake the next. Fresh fruit, coffee, and tea come with every breakfast.

Ten Inverness Way is located just off Sir Francis Drake (the main street that runs through town). From the inn you can reach the village shops, restaurants, and Point Reyes National Seashore on foot. Golden Gate Transit provides service between San Francisco and Inverness; the bus stop is a block from the house.

Byron Randall's Guest House

25 Valley Street
Tomales, California 94971; (707) 878-9992

INNKEEPER:	*Byron Randall.*
ACCOMMODATIONS:	*Eight rooms, one with private bath; twin and double beds.*
RESERVATIONS:	*Two weeks recommended.*
MINIMUM STAY:	*None.*
DEPOSIT:	*Full amount.*
CREDIT CARDS:	*Not accepted.*
RATES:	*Inexpensive.*
RESTRICTIONS:	*No children under ten. No pets.*

I didn't see Byron Randall the entire time I was at his "famous Victorian Tomales guest house and art gallery." Neither did any of his other guests. It was rumored that he was in Seattle (or was it Vancouver?). No one seemed to know, no one seemed to care. The clientele (many of them "regulars") seemed to like Byron's laissez-faire way of doing business just fine.

Byron perfected his "absentee" system of inn-keeping after years in the business. (He is credited with opening the first guest house on the Mendocino coast some twenty years ago; he's been at the Tomales address for the past ten years.) The system, though confusing at first, is really quite simple: you sign yourself in, pick out the room you want, take the corresponding room key from a pegboard in the hall, and then make yourself right at home.

The house, a redwood Victorian, was built in 1899. Oldtimers in the area (Swiss and Italian immigrants who settled here to develop the dairy business) refer to it as the "old Restano place," the showplace of its day. The size of the house makes it a natural as an inn. There are eight bedrooms. Each is furnished differently, but all the furnishings were salvaged from houses of the same time period. The upstairs rooms have beams and slanted ceilings as well as views of the garden. One of the downstairs rooms (with windows that face east to catch the morning sun) formerly served as Byron's studio. All the rooms display his paintings.

One of the weekend guests best described Byron's: "inexpensive (from $35), low key, and completely anonymous." A dozen or so other reasons to visit his guest house include the library, which is well stocked with books and games (there's also a fireplace and a piano), a fully equipped kitchen (its use is strongly encouraged), the outdoor patio, bullfrogs in the lily pond, white owls and chickens, blue jays and pathways, peace and quiet, and a friendly next-door neighbor. The house is two miles from Tomales Bay, ten minutes from Dillon Beach, and not far from the Russian River, Point Reyes National Seashore, and California's famed wine country.

Heretofore breakfast has consisted of strong coffee and "bring/cook your own." But in a telephone interview with Byron (yes, there really is a Byron) he informed me that he was instituting a light Continental breakfast: English muffins with sweet butter and jam and fresh fruit to go along with the strong coffee.

I'll be checking back. Hope to meet you soon, Byron.

Chalet Bed and Breakfast

18935 Fifth Street West
Sonoma, California 95476; (707) 996-0190

INNKEEPERS:	*Patrick and Lolita Murphy.*
ACCOMMODATIONS:	*Four rooms share two baths;*
	double beds.
RESERVATIONS:	*Four weeks recommended.*
MINIMUM STAY:	*None.*
DEPOSIT:	*In full.*
CREDIT CARDS:	*MC, VISA.*
RATES:	*Moderate.*
RESTRICTIONS:	*No pets.*

I t was late when I pulled into Sonoma. "The Murphys have probably given up on me by now," I thought to myself as I fumbled around for the street map. At just about the same moment I crossed Fifth Street, but there was no sign of the Chalet — or anything resembling a bed and breakfast inn. I pulled the establishment's card out of my purse. " . . . overnite accommodations in a wonderful country farm setting . . . " Fifth Street didn't look like a "country farm setting" to me. I saw trailer courts and tract houses, gas stations and shopping centers, but no sign of "the country." Exasperated, I pulled up to a pay phone in Safeway's parking lot. "Hello, Lolita? H-E-L-P!"

All's well that ends well, so they say. And let me be the first to tell you that Fifth Street ends well — well up a one-lane dirt road. And yes, the Chalet, the first bed and breakfast to open in Sonoma, is situated in a country-like setting, complete with chickens and goats.

The house is a two-story Swiss chalet built in 1940. It is furnished with a mix of country antiques and collectibles: 1920 radios, patchwork quilts, wicker furniture, cast-iron stoves, Navajo rugs, an antique doll collection, and California pottery.

Accommodations consist of two downstairs bedrooms that share a bath and a sitting room, and two upstairs rooms with a shared bath. The upstairs parlor has a wood-burning stove and limited kitchen facilities. There's an extra bed for a child or a third adult in one of the downstairs rooms. The overall feel reflects Lolita's personal preference for "antiques, comfort, and good food."

Speaking of good food, the innkeepers offer a hearty, farm-style breakfast that starts off with freshly squeezed orange juice, a fruit cup, sausage and eggs (or the "omelette of the day"), a home-baked walnut coffee cake, and French-roast coffee. Fresh fruits and vegetables from the garden and eggs from the chickens are on the menu.

The Chalet is located in the Valley of the Moon, a fascinating area steeped in early California history and surrounded by wineries and vineyards. Sonoma's central plaza (a great place to sightsee, shop, and picnic) is just three quarters of a mile from the inn. The town bakery, a cheese factory, and a sausage shop supply all the makings for a picnic on the square or at nearby Jack London State Park.

Pygmalion House

331 Orange Street
Santa Rosa, California 95401; (707) 526-3407

INNKEEPER:	*Lola Wright.*
ACCOMMODATIONS:	*Three rooms, all with shared bath; twin, double, and king-size beds.*
RESERVATIONS:	*Two weeks recommended.*
MINIMUM STAY:	*None.*
DEPOSIT:	*First night's lodging.*
CREDIT CARDS:	*Not accepted.*
RATES:	*Inexpensive to moderate.*
RESTRICTIONS:	*No pets.*

Santa Rosa was never on my "top ten" list of places to visit in California. But since I was searching out bed and breakfast inns and had heard that one had recently opened there, I thought I'd stop by. I spotted a beautifully restored (and freshly painted) Victorian from the freeway and something (perhaps intuition, perhaps experience) told me that if there was a b&b in Santa Rosa this was it. I followed directions a friend had jotted down: Downtown exit from 101. Third Street to Wilson. Left turn. One block to Hazel. Another left. A right onto Orange. Last house on the right. It came as no surprise that the last house on the right and the house I saw from the freeway were one and the same: Pygmalion House.

The house is a classic example of what one expects of a bed and breakfast. It has charm and history. And, from a typical bed and breakfast enthusiast's point of view, it's just the right size.

Three bedrooms share two baths. Each room is named for the predominant color of its decor. The Blue Room wins my vote of approval: blue and white flowered wallpaper, plush blue carpeting, French Provincial furnishings, lace curtains, and a king-size bed. The bathroom has an old-fashioned claw-foot tub with brass fixtures.

Guests enjoy a full breakfast (brought to the room on request). A sample menu: corn flakes or granola, fresh fruit in season, yogurt, date-nut muffins, coffee, and freshly squeezed orange juice. Other amenities: the morning paper, fresh flowers in the room, and sherry in the parlor in the afternoon.

Lola Wright brings her twenty-five years of experience staying at b&b's throughout Europe and ten years as manager of an inn in Hawaii to Pygmalion House. Accordingly she defines her innkeeping style as incorporating some European comfort and attention with Southern hospitality and lots of Aloha spirit.

Pygmalion House is adjacent to Railroad Square, the historical part of Santa Rosa that is rapidly gaining popularity for its shops and fine restaurants. And (as I discovered) Santa Rosa is central to many areas of interest: the Napa and Sonoma wine country, the Russian River, San Francisco, Point Reyes National Seashore, and the ocean.

Green Apple Inn

520 Bohemian Highway
Freestone, California; (707) 874-2526

INNKEEPERS:	*Rogers and Rosemary Hoffman.*
ACCOMMODATIONS:	*Four rooms share two baths; twin and double beds.*
RESERVATIONS:	*Two weeks recommended.*
MINIMUM STAY:	*Two nights on weekends during the summer; two nights over holiday periods.*
DEPOSIT:	*First night's lodging.*
CREDIT CARDS:	*Not accepted.*
RATES:	*Moderate.*
RESTRICTIONS:	*No children under seven.*

I n the late nineteenth century two brothers, joint owners of one of the original homes in the town of Freestone, had a serious falling out. The burning issue has long since been forgotten, but the consequence remains. Showing more logic than rationality, one brother sawed off his half of the house and took it elsewhere. Astonished, the other brother rolled in another house and tacked it on to the wounded building.

Although the general consensus within the village is that this story is true, there is some strong difference of opinion as to which of the Freestone homes the story applies.

Rogers and Rosemary Hoffman, proprietors of the Green Apple Inn, invite you to note the different structural styles within their home and share the conviction that, indeed, it is this house that is the result of the historic occurrence.

The Hoffmans' Green Apple Inn is located on five acres of meadowland and redwood groves. Its sitting room, four guest rooms, and two baths provide an intimate atmosphere for socializing and spinning a few yarns of one's own. Heirlooms and family treasures fill the house, the most unusual of these are Rogers' great-grandfather's Civil War gun (a portrait of the late Thomas Rogers hangs above the fireplace mantel), the one-hundred-year-old Seth Thomas mantel clock, a Japanese wood carving, a coal scuttle from the turn of the century, a French Revolution—era etching, and a 250-year-old brass coffee urn. (Guest rooms hold iron and brass beds with fluffy patchwork and floral-print comforters, marble-topped dressers, wicker pieces, and wild flowers.)

As expected, apple-based dishes make up the breakfast menu at the Green Apple Inn. Typical fare includes French toast with walnuts and apples, a fresh-fruit salad or baked apple in wintertime, freshly baked apple bread with homemade marmalade, and coffee.

After breakfast you can take a walking tour of Freestone's award-winning nursery, visit the local bird farm, homespun clothing store, or metal sculpture workshop, hike through the surrounding hills and valleys, or tell your troubles to Maude, the Hoffmans' pet nanny goat. Bicycles are courtesy of the inn.

Ridenhour Ranch House Inn

12850 River Road
Guerneville, California 95446; (707) 887-1033

INNKEEPERS:	*Bob and Martha Satterthwaite.*
ACCOMMODATIONS:	*Seven rooms, four with private bath; double and queen-size beds.*
RESERVATIONS:	*Four weeks recommended.*
MINIMUM STAY:	*Two nights on weekends and holidays.*
DEPOSIT:	*First night's lodging.*
CREDIT CARDS:	*MC, VISA.*
RATES:	*Moderate.*
RESTRICTIONS:	*Children: Minimum age ten. No pets.*

Louis William Ridenhour was a homesteader from Missouri who came to California in 1850 and in 1856 began to farm the Ridenhour Ranch — 940 acres on both sides of the Russian River. In 1906 his son, Louis E. Ridenhour, constructed a handsome ranch house of heart redwood on 2¼ acres of the property. The younger Ridenhour's daughter Virginia, and her husband, former Assistant Surgeon General Justin K. Fuller, eventually came into possession of the house, and in 1954 they enlarged and improved it.

Martha and Bob Satterthwaite purchased the home in 1977 and worked for two years remodeling it into a bed and breakfast inn patterned after those they had discovered on trips through the western part of the United States and Europe. The result, Ridenhour Ranch House Inn, is one of the finest inns this side of the eastern seaboard.

This two-story, eleven-room house has seven bedrooms, a large country kitchen, and a formal dining room. The comfortable living room beckons guests to relax, chat, read, play cards, put together a puzzle, or just sit and sip a glass of wine in front of the brick fireplace.

Each bedroom is individually and tastefully appointed with country English and American antique furnishings, quilts, oriental rugs, the finest-quality linens, flowers, and plants. The bathroom medicine cabinets are stocked with toothpaste, Band-Aids, and other essentials one might have left behind.

A complimentary breakfast of freshly ground coffee, juice, hot rolls and nut breads, fruit, and cheese is served each morning in the kitchen or the dining room. Trays are available for guests to take breakfast back to their room or out to the patio.

The informally landscaped grounds invite a stroll under the redwoods and oaks. The trees of the orchard yield a variety of fruit (apples, peaches, pears, and figs) for picking and eating. A hot tub is available for guests' use. Secluded river beaches are a short walk away. One can walk to Korbel Winery for a tour of their champagne cellars.

Something to note: the inn is closed to the public during the months of December and January.

Grape Leaf Inn

539 Johnson Street
Healdsburg, California 95448; (707) 433-8140

INNKEEPERS:	*Terry Sweet and Kathy Cookson.*
ACCOMMODATIONS:	*Seven rooms, all with private bath; queen- and king-size beds. Wheelchair access.*
RESERVATIONS:	*Three to six weeks recommended.*
MINIMUM STAY:	*Two nights on weekends.*
DEPOSIT:	*First night's lodging.*
CREDIT CARDS:	*MC, VISA.*
RATES:	*Moderate.*
RESTRICTIONS:	*No children under twelve. No pets.*

I liked Grape Leaf Inn when it was owned by Laura Salo, but I like it even more now that the new owner, Terry Sweet, has remodeled, expanded, and transformed this cute Queen Anne into a seven-bedroom, seven-bath gem that is surely the envy of the competition.

The inn is located in the small town of Healdsburg, a short bike ride from one of California's premier grape-growing regions: the Alexander Valley.

In keeping with the natural surroundings, the proprietor has named the guest rooms after grape varietals: Merlot, Pinot Noir, Gamay Rose. Cabernet Sauvignon has skylight windows in both bedroom and bath. The Chardonnay Suite features stained-glass windows, an antique armoire, and a separate sitting room; there's an old-fashioned pull-chain toilet and a double-sink oak vanity in the bath. Sauvignon Blanc's brass and iron bed faces a bay window with a love seat. And the Zinfandel Room has a king-size bed, an antique oak dresser, and an Oriental rug that covers the hardwood floor. (The four upstairs rooms all have sloped roofs and two-person whirlpool tub/showers.)

Innkeeper Kathy Cookson pours a sampling of Sonoma County wine to go along with the Sonoma County cheeses that are served in the front parlor late each afternoon. Books, magazines, and games are available, or one can just sit and relax on the sofa in front of the fireplace. A collection of local artists' paintings and photographs are on display throughout the inn.

A full country breakfast is served buffet style from 8:30 to 10:00 in the dining room. Featured dishes include Mexican eggs with guacamole, bacon and broccoli frittata, or quiche Lorraine, fresh blueberry or banana-almond coffee cake (the inn's most requested recipe), cereal and milk, fresh fruit in season, (baked apples in winter), freshly ground coffee and freshly squeezed orange juice.

Within walking distance of the inn are river beaches and night-lighted tennis courts. Bicycles can be rented just three blocks away for informal tours of the wine country. The innkeeper will make dinner reservations or arrangements for river canoe trips and other recreational activities.

Something else to note: room rates are discounted midweek from November to March.

Belle de Jour

16276 Healdsburg Avenue
Healdsburg, California 95448; (707) 433-7892

INNKEEPER:	*Custis Piper.*
ACCOMMODATIONS:	*Five rooms, one with private bath; twin, double, queen-, and king-size beds.*
RESERVATIONS:	*Two weeks recommended.*
MINIMUM STAY:	*None.*
DEPOSIT:	*$50.*
CREDIT CARDS:	*Not accepted.*
RATES:	*Moderate.*
RESTRICTIONS:	*No children. No pets.*

When Custis Piper visits an inn there are three questions she asks: What's it like? What's to eat? And what's to do? Custis not only frequents inns, she owns and operates one: Belle de Jour, one of the three bed and breakfasts located in the wine country town of Healdsburg.

A visitor to *her* inn would have little difficulty answering the first of these three questions. What's it like? Exactly like a weekend visit to a farm, replete with goats, chickens, rabbits, and sheep. The farmhouse — a Victorian that was built sometime around 1875 — sits among six acres of fruit-bearing trees (pear, plum, and prune, to name a few). The atmosphere is informal, and as this is Ms. Piper's home as well as her single-handed commercial enterprise, the furnishings suit her taste. Included are Tiffany lamps and Victorian antiques, as well as antiques of other periods. The dining room features a fireplace, the living room a piano. Guest quarters include a large bedroom with a queen-size bed, a small room with a double bed (these rooms share the hall bath), a double with a king-size bed and a private bath, and two separate cottages overlooking the back meadow. For those with a real spirit of adventure, the recently remodeled bunkhouse (with a kitchenette and full bath) accommodates three overnight guests.

What's to eat? The emphasis is on home-grown, farm-fresh foods. Incorporated into the day's menu are fresh fruits, home-baked coffee cakes and croissants, fresh butter, eggs, and milk.

What's to do? That depends on your taste — and your energy level. The number one preference among the regular clientele is "absolutely nothing." For the more ambitious, field trips, tours of local wineries, bicycle tours, and picnics (a basket lunch is provided for a slight charge with advance notice) are all possibilities. There's the porch swing and (according to Custis) plenty of weeds that need pulling around the place.

Belle de Jour is open Wednesday through Sunday by reservation only. From Highway 101 take the Dry Creek Road off ramp. Turn right on Dry Creek to the stoplight; left on Healdsburg Avenue and continue for approximately one mile. The Simi Winery tasting room is on the left, Belle de Jour on the right.

Campbell Ranch Inn

1475 Canyon Road
Geyserville, California 95441; (707) 857-3476

INNKEEPERS:	*Mary Jane and Jerry Campbell.*
ACCOMMODATIONS:	*Three rooms, one with private bath; king-size beds.*
RESERVATIONS:	*Two to three weeks recommended.*
MINIMUM STAY:	*Two nights on weekends.*
DEPOSIT:	*Half of full amount.*
CREDIT CARDS:	*Not accepted.*
RATES:	*Moderate.*
RESTRICTIONS:	*No children. No pets.*

 generous man will prosper; he who refreshes others will himself be refreshed.

Proverbs 11:25

I not only feel right at home at the Campbell Ranch, I feel as though I could return again and again. This is due in part to the serenity here. Perhaps it is also due to the fact that since the Campbell's living quarters are not separate from their inn operation, one immediately feels like part of the family. Then again it might just have something to do with that delicious banana cream pie (my favorite) that is served at the kitchen table just before bedtime. But no one describes the Campbell Ranch experience better than Mary Jane when she says, "People come here to *stay!*"

There's plenty more to stay for — picturesque hilltop views of lush rolling vineyards, a well-maintained swimming pool, tennis courts, horseshoes, Ping-Pong, and billiards, not to mention bicycles and peaceful country roads.

The Campbell Ranch is a modern, split-level ranch-style home with traditional furnishings. The living room's two floral-patterned sofas sit face-to-face in front of a massive brick fireplace that divides the living room from the family room, where guests find chess, checkers, jigsaw puzzles, a stereo, and yes, even a television set.

The bedroom on the lower level (Room A) affords the most privacy, as it is the sole bedroom on this floor and the only one available with a private bath. Here you will find wood-paneled walls, green plants, a desk, and a comfortable reading chair, as well as a collection of *National Geographic* magazines that date from 1959 — enough to keep an armchair traveler holed-up here for years.

My favorite room was the one I stayed in overnight — preselected from the brochure for its Baldwin piano and balcony with a view of the countryside — Room B. There was a spacious closet, a desk, ivy plants, and shelves abounding with good reading material.

Mary Jane cites her job as a maid during her college years and her experience as a wife and mother (three boys, in ages ranging from sixteen to twenty-one) as the training ground for operating a bed and breakfast inn.

"Jerry's the handyman around here," she says. "He does all the grass cutting and repairs — though he loves socializing too. He is genuinely interested in people, and a good conversationalist."

The kitchen provides the setting for breakfast, which is served until 10:00 A.M. Monday through Saturday and until 9:00 A.M. on Sundays. Selections include a choice of cantaloupe with fresh strawberries, *or* freshly squeezed orange juice, *or* orange halves, *or* sliced bananas with sugar and cream. Group B consists of cold cereal, a cheese omelet, fried eggs and potatoes, or the Campbell Ranch egg puff (loaded with fresh sautéed mushrooms and Monterey Jack cheese). From "Group C" you can choose between white toast, zucchini bread, carrot cake, sour cream coffee cake, homemade honey-wheat loaf, or bran muffins. And finally, the beverages: coffee, tea, milk, or hot chocolate.

There's plenty to do after breakfast for those who aren't content to just *stay*: winery tours, a nearby dam and fish hatchery, and canoeing or tubing on the Russian River (just seven minutes away). Snoopyland, home of cartoonist Charles Shultz, is in nearby Santa Rosa. The inn also provides a central location for easy day trips to Mendocino, Napa, Sonoma, and even San Francisco.

The Hope-Merrill House

21253 Geyserville Avenue, P.O. Box 42
Geyserville, California 95441; (707) 857-3356

INNKEEPERS:	*Bob and Rosalie Hope.*
ACCOMMODATIONS:	*Five rooms, two with private bath; double and queen-size beds.*
RESERVATIONS:	*Three to four weeks recommended.*
MINIMUM STAY:	*None.*
DEPOSIT:	*First night's lodging.*
CREDIT CARDS:	*MC, VISA.*
RATES:	*Moderate.*
RESTRICTIONS:	*No children. No pets.*

V ictoriana buffs arise — and head straight to Geyserville, for one of the finest overnight experiences on the bed and breakfast circuit — the Hope-Merrill House, named after present-day owners/innkeepers Bob and Rosalie Hope, and the original builder/occupant, J.P. Merrill.

This 1875-ish Eastlake/Stick Style Victorian is a virtual museum of the trends and treasures of its time, from the carefully researched and reproduced wall coverings to the period furnishings and fixtures. Of special interest is the Lincrusta-Walton wainscoting in the entranceway and upstairs hall, and the tin ceiling in the kitchen. The Hopes' collection of glassware and bric-a-brac, as well as their books on Victorian gardens, furnishings, and house building (and one on gas lighting in America), delight the eye and captivate the mind.

The reasonably priced guest accommodations include the Victorian Room with its old trunk, chaise longue, antique perfume bottles, and walnut carved headboard from the 1860s; the Peacock Room, the only downstairs bedroom with a fireplace and a queen-size bed; the Briar Rose Room, in shades of pink and rose; the Bachelor's Button, with a brass bed, chestnut dresser, and Maxfield Parrish prints; and the Carpenter Gothic Room, which shares a bath down the hall.

Victoriana buffs awake — to one of the most delicious gourmet breakfasts found on the bed and breakfast circuit. Rosalie (a caterer whose creations are highly respected by the top names in the Valley) is known for her hot poached pears with ginger, fresh peaches with zabaglione, chili egg puff with salsa, French toast like no other, sour cream coffee cake, homemade apple butter, and homemade jams.

The slow-paced, rural atmosphere makes one inclined to linger, perhaps too long, while scenic views along Highway 128 and tours and tastings along the Russian River Wine Road await. Bob offers wine-tasting advice and cites this, along with lovemaking, as the two activities his guests seem to be most interested in — "canoeing runs a distant third," he adds.

"Our desire was to authentically re-create a living history of the Victorian era for people to enjoy," Bob explains. Victoriana buffs acclaim: Well done!

Vintage Towers

302 North Main Street
Cloverdale, California 95425; (707) 894-4535

INNKEEPERS:	Tom and Judy Haworth.
ACCOMMODATIONS:	Seven rooms, five with private bath; double, queen-, and king-size beds.
RESERVATIONS:	Three weeks recommended.
MINIMUM STAY:	Two nights on weekends, May through September.
DEPOSIT:	First night's lodging.
CREDIT CARDS:	MC, VISA.
RATES:	Inexpensive to moderate.
RESTRICTIONS:	Children: Minimum age ten. No pets.

L onging for the days when sitting on the porch swing with a glass of ice-cold lemonade was considered part of the American way of life? Wishing you could get away to a small town with a pace far removed from that of the city? Well, there's Vintage Towers, a grand Queen Anne Victorian located just a block east of Highway 101 in the town of Cloverdale.

This twenty-room mansion (built at the turn of the century by Simon Pinshcower, a wealthy Cloverdale merchant who aspired to own the biggest house in town) is owned and operated as a bed and breakfast inn by Tom and Judy Haworth. This hard-working but fun-loving couple managed to turn the house into the town's showplace as well as its showpiece.

The house has three working fireplaces, a library with over one thousand volumes, and a music room with a player piano, all for the guests' enjoyment. The seven bedrooms (each architecturally unusual) are furnished with period pieces and named after their individual decor and theme; there's Scarlett's Room, Bordello Burgundy, the Calico Tower (three of the accommodations are tower suites), and the Carousel Tower Suite, complete with a carousel horse and original circus posters.

The Haworths' individual traits and talents are part

of the attraction. Tom has a knack for making people feel right at home (he's from a family of nine!), and Judy (a home economics major) is a whiz in the kitchen. Her weekday breakfasts are simple but delicious: fresh fruit compote, homemade nut breads and muffins, and orange juice and coffee. Although I didn't sample the weekend menu first-hand, it's said to be a bit more substantial; Sunday champagne brunch features entrées ranging from soufflés to eggs Benedict.

Cloverdale, a quiet New England–like town, affords one the pleasure of strolling past old houses and stately churches on tree-lined streets. Within minutes of the inn are many wineries, including Italian Swiss Colony. Secluded beaches and hiking trails are nearby. A half-day excursion might include a visit to the world-renowned geysers; a day-long journey begins down the Russian River Wine Road that starts in Cloverdale and goes all the way to Korbel Champagne Cellars near Guerneville.

Vintage Towers provides bicycles; canoes can be reserved locally. The Haworths own a twenty-five-foot sailing sloop that can be reserved for an afternoon on the nearby lake, and Tom can arrange an action-packed tubing trip down the Russian River.

BORDEAUX HOUSE

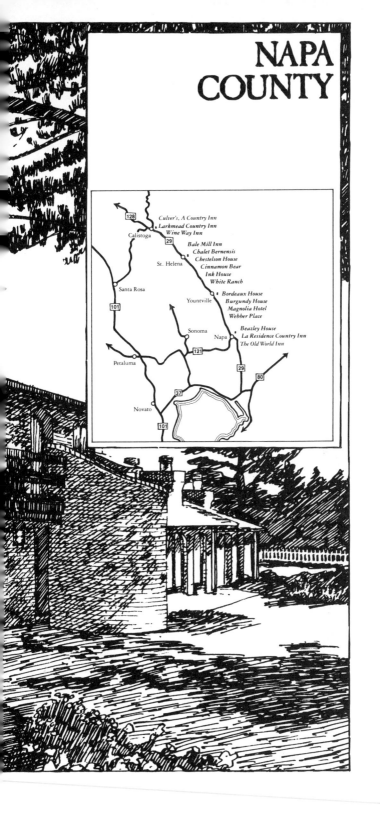

NAPA COUNTY

Culver's, A Country Inn
Larkmead Country Inn
Wine Way Inn

Calistoga

Bale Mill Inn
Chalet Bernensis
Chestelson House
Cinnamon Bear
Ink House
White Ranch

St. Helena

Santa Rosa

Bordeaux House
Burgundy House
Magnolia Hotel
Webber Place

Yountville

Sonoma

Beazley House
La Residence Country Inn
The Old World Inn

Napa

Petaluma

Novato

Beazley House

1910 First Street
Napa, California 94558; (707) 257-1649

INNKEEPERS:	Jim and Carol Beazley.
ACCOMMODATIONS:	Eight rooms, private and shared baths; queen-size beds.
RESERVATIONS:	Two to three weeks recommended.
MINIMUM STAY:	Two nights on weekends.
DEPOSIT:	First night's lodging.
CREDIT CARDS:	MC, VISA.
RATES:	Expensive.
RESTRICTIONS:	No children under twelve. No pets.

Fond memories of the Beazley House: friendly people (Jim and Carol Beazley), the smell of freshly baked muffins wafting from the kitchen, a warm and snuggly down comforter, and one of the finest old homes in Napa (an early California town with more than its share of distinguished literary and business personalities).

This two-story, Colonial Revival/Shingle-style house was built in 1902. Its hardwood floors, wainscoting, cove ceilings, and stained-glass windows bespeak its Edwardian origins. There's a large living room with a fireplace and a window flanked by bookshelves. (The Beazleys also keep plenty of games on hand: backgammon, chess, Yatzee, and dominoes are all available.) To the right of the music room is the formal dining room, where a breakfast of fresh fruits, home-baked muffins or bread and jams, coffee and tea, and fruit juice is served beginning promptly at 8:30 each morning. Guest rooms are individually decorated and named according to theme. In addition to the three accommodations in the main house, the Carriage House provides five rooms with fireplaces and private baths. (The loft rooms have two-person spas.)

The Beazleys are as comfortable and accommodating as their house. Both are unabashedly people-oriented. Carol served as a full-time nurse for fourteen years; Jim was a photo-journalist with the *Reno Evening Gazette* and *Nevada State Journal.* A tour of b&b's in England and California left them with a confirmed belief in the owner-occupant philosophy of innkeeping. Many a stranger leaves Beazley House a friend — perhaps because this inn is a home as well as a business for its owners.

Beazley House is three blocks from central Napa, a city that is experiencing a rebirth as a tourist destination. It offers historic-architectural walking tours within the immediate area. There is also hot-air ballooning, cycling, gliding, horseback riding, and the Robert L. Stevenson Museum, all within a few miles. With its bright blue and white awnings, balanced symmetry and gracefully hipped roof, visitors will have no difficulty finding this attractive wine country inn. (It will soon be listed in the National Register of Historic Places.) But despite its impressive exterior, the best memories most people take away are of the warm and familylike atmosphere within. "We treat each individual not just as a customer," say the Beazleys, "but as a guest."

La Residence Country Inn

4066 St. Helena Highway North
Napa, California 94558; (707) 253-0337

INNKEEPER:	Barbara Littenberg.
ACCOMMODATIONS:	Fifteen rooms, twelve with private bath; queen-size beds.
RESERVATIONS:	Two to four weeks recommended.
MINIMUM STAY:	Two nights on weekends.
DEPOSIT:	In full.
CREDIT CARDS:	AE, MC, VISA.
RATES:	Moderate to expensive.
RESTRICTIONS:	No children. No pets.

Harry C. Parker was a river pilot in New Orleans in the 1840s who caught gold fever and arrived in San Francisco in 1849. A merchant in Stockton and San Francisco, he moved to Napa County in 1865 and took up farming. In 1870 he built his dream house, a Gothic Revival with a distinctly Southern flavor. Today his home still projects this amalgamation of regional styles, and the clientele attracted by its modern-day owners reflects the adventurous spirit of its original creator and inhabitant.

There is elegance here, as befits a home built by a man from the land of magnolias. Proprietor Barbara Littenberg has gone out of her way to furnish the rooms with antiques of the nineteenth century. (Her background as both fashion designer and archaeologist clearly is in evidence here.) The main library is well stocked with mysteries, with a preponderance of the English drawing room genre. (One room boasts a small library containing the works of Robert Louis Stevenson, the nineteenth-century English literary light who lived nearby.) Indeed, Barbara professes a strong preference for the English style of innkeeping, citing the White Moss Inn in the Lake District as the hostelry that has most influenced her own operation.

Bicycle enthusiasts will find a bike trail beginning right across the road. (It runs all the way to Yountville.)

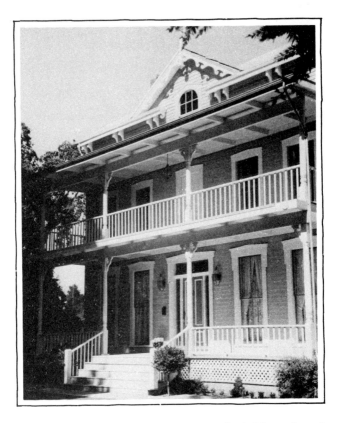

Runners are encouraged to enjoy the fresh Napa air and sunshine on the same trail. Balloonists frequently stay here because of the proximity of the ballooning facilities, and the Littenbergs are happy to recommend tours at the local wineries. But if it's simply rest and relaxation you thirst after, you will not be disappointed. Each bedroom has its own sitting area, and the parklike setting gives the entire area a secluded and restful ambience. Its two acres boast magnolias (naturally), California live oaks, and orange, walnut, fig, apple, and pear trees.

The Continental breakfast of orange juice (fresh), coffee, croissants, and fresh fruit is served from 8:30 to 10:00 in the dining room. But you may find evenings at La Residence just as enjoyable; the Littenbergs are especially interested in serving an international clientele. "That's the part I like best," says Barbara. "Sitting around the parlor in the evening, sharing stories from all over the world." I'm sure the footloose Harry C. would approve.

The Old World Inn

1301 Jefferson Street
Napa, California 94559; (707) 257-0112

INNKEEPERS:	*Geoffrey and Janet Villiers.*
ACCOMMODATIONS:	*Eight rooms, all with private bath; twin, double, queen-, and king-size beds.*
RESERVATIONS:	*Two to three weeks recommended.*
MINIMUM STAY:	*Two nights on weekends.*
DEPOSIT:	*First night's lodging.*
CREDIT CARDS:	*AE, MC, VISA.*
RATES:	*Moderate to expensive.*
RESTRICTIONS:	*No children. No pets.*

hen Macy's prepared to launch their China Seas collection they chose Napa's Old World Inn to show off the color-coordinated fabrics and linens. So the Old World Inn interiors are courtesy of Macy's, but the Old World Inn charm is courtesy of Geoffrey and Janet Villiers, the gracious and good-humored proprietors recently transplanted here from the southwest of England.

The art of innkeeping is not new to the Villiers, in fact you could say they perfected it at their Country House inn in Somerset County prior to settling in the Napa Valley. "A blissfully happy life" is how they describe their life as innkeepers. A refreshing attitude, this — and one that makes even more sense combined with the following commet: "We're retired, you see, so now we're doing exactly what we want, because we enjoy it — not because we have to."

The Villiers residence (painted a vintner's leaf green with grape trim) was built by Napa contractor E.W. Doughty in 1906. Its shingle siding, wide shady porches, clinker brick, and leaded- and beveled-glass windows reveal an eclectic combination of architectural styles.

Bright Scandinavian colors and a mix of painted Victorian and antique furniture dominate the inn's parlor and eight guest rooms, which were inspired by Swedish artist Carl Larsson. Cotton-candy-colored bows, trailing vines, and other fanciful designs are painted around the border of the walls and up the hallway, where stenciled lettering announces the name of each room: Carl Larsson's Room, Inger's Room, Anne's Room, the Mint Room, the Blue Room, the Birch Room, and the Garden Room. The most popular room in the house is the downstairs Stockholm Room, with its multicolored striped fabric and a private entrance off the veranda.

Among the features enchancing the guests' comfort are the air conditioning in summer and the large custom Jacuzzi shaped like a cluster of grapes.

Tea and shortbread greets guests on arrival, a cheese board with hot French bread is set out after 5:00, and yummy chocolate-fudge cake and homemade peppermints satisfy that urge for a "little something" just before bedtime.

Webber Place

6610 Webber Street, P.O. Box 2873
Yountville, California 94599; (707) 944-8384

INNKEEPERS:	*Diane Bartholomew and Patsy Gordon.*
ACCOMMODATIONS:	*Four rooms, two with private bath; double beds.*
RESERVATIONS:	*Three weeks recommended.*
MINIMUM STAY:	*None.*
DEPOSIT:	*First night's lodging.*
CREDIT CARDS:	*MC, VISA.*
RATES:	*Moderate to expensive.*
RESTRICTIONS:	*No children. No pets.*

ebber Place is a 1½-story Greek Revival farmhouse. And what a farmhouse! This is the storybook clapboard farmhouse *par excellence*, complete with a delicate white picket fence. Built by Sylvester and Polly Grigsby (descendants of Capt. John Grigsby of the Bear Flag Revolt) in the 1850s, it was moved to its present station by one of the industrious Webber clan in the latter part of that decade. Loren Holte began work on this "piece of junk that nobody wanted" in the early 1970s. He reconstructed almost the entire interior of this historic rust-red dwelling, while preserving many of the original accoutrements. (These include newspaper clippings from around the turn of the century, which were framed and put on the walls; they were discovered during renovation.)

One of several small miracles of reconstruction: over the years the wood paneling on the ceiling had been painted over several times. Each panel was simply flipped over and carefully reattached to the wood surface. The result was the intricate tongue and groove redwood paneling that graces many of the ceilings (and one wall) of the rooms.

The town of Yountville, in which Webber Place is located, is itself a small miracle of reconstruction. It was nothing more than a sleepy village containing a Veterans Hospital until a few years ago. Then Vintage 1870 — an attractive oasis of shops and boutiques — was opened by enterprising locals with an eye to attracting more of the tourist dollar. Employment went up, and the area received a face lift that in turn attracted other business catering to tourism. It now boasts four inns, several fine restaurants, and the Court of Two Sisters bakery.

Webber Place-isms I particularly liked: guests are greeted with wine from local wineries, such as Mondavi or Round Hill. There are fresh flowers in the rooms, and most rooms have old-fashioned, claw-foot bathtubs (some built for two, yet) on raised platforms, and pull-chain water closets. The lower suite is perfect for honeymooners, opening onto its private veranda with a private entrance as well. Wine and perishables may be stored in the refrigerator by guests; the Continental breakfast often includes homemade breads (the zucchini and the banana are both yummy).

Patsy Gordon and Diane Bartholomew purchased the property from Loren Holte in June of 1983, and to the delight of inngoers they have established a few traditions all their own: freshly squeezed lemonade and old-fashioned sun tea, homemade oatmeal cookies, and mom's hot apple pie.

Future plans call for a gazebo in the backyard, a swimming pool fashioned to look like a reflecting pond, a hot tub, and an addition with four new rooms. Webber Place will be an interesting inn to keep an eye on.

Magnolia Hotel

6529 Yount Street
Yountville, California 94599; (707) 944-2056

INNKEEPERS:	*Bruce and Bonnie Locken.*
ACCOMMODATIONS:	*Eleven rooms, all with private bath; double, queen-, and king-size beds.*
RESERVATIONS:	*Two to three months for weekends.*
MINIMUM STAY:	*None.*
DEPOSIT:	*First and last night's lodging.*
CREDIT CARDS:	*Not accepted.*
RATES:	*Moderate to expensive.*
RESTRICTIONS:	*No children under sixteen. No pets.*

I t was built as a hotel in 1873, of brick and native fieldstone — reputedly from the Silverado Trail. In the intervening years it has been a bordello, a hotel for laborers, a 4-H headquarters, and a speakeasy during Prohibition. It was rescued from oblivion by Ray and Nancy Monte (two of the creators of Vintage 1870) and is now owned by Bonnie and Bruce Locken, who have turned the Magnolia Hotel into one of the classiest and most fashionable country inns in the vineyards of California.

Class tells right from the moment one enters and spies the antique rolltop desk in the lobby. There is a formal parlor; the second floor has a very large deck, perfect for sipping wine and looking out over the surrounding vineyards. (The wine cellar is stocked with over three hundred California wines.)

Each room has its own handmade theme doll created by Bonnie especially for that room. In the Magnolia Room I discovered a private balcony overlooking the heated pool. (I also found a welcome decanter of port wine.) There is a heated Jacuzzi with a redwood deck in the rear. My bedspread pattern was cleverly keyed to correspond to wall decor, and I liked the fireplace, the needlepoint chair design, and the pink lace curtains. (Other rooms have iron and brass beds, handmade quilts, and lace coverlets.) All rooms have a private tiled bath and plush towels, and it is worth noting that the Magnolia is air-conditioned during the summer.

Bruce Locken has long been in the hostelry trade, serving for thirty years at famous spots such as San Francisco's Clift Hotel. But he yearned for something different. "I wanted to get back to the small, intimate kind of operation — which is really how the business began," he says. He searched for eight years. In 1977 he found the Magnolia already in operation. It was love at first sight.

Bonnie is in charge of the kitchen, as one would expect from a professional who worked as a dietician for a chain of western hospitals.

For breakfast enjoy French toast baked in rounds; hot port wine syrup (they make it); sausage or double-thick bacon, from California Meat Company, one of the oldest sausage makers in San Francisco; fresh orange juice and eggs, baked or as an omelette (try New York sharp Cheddar cheese with mushrooms and sherry wine); and old-fashioned oatmeal with brown sugar, banana chips, and cream. (The breakfast is served "family style" in the adjacent dining room.)

If you can break away from the Lockens' famous collection of cookbooks, nearby attractions include a petrified forest, over a hundred wineries, a geyser named Old Faithful after its prototype in Yellowstone, and a mud bath (yes, a mud bath). The Lockens are happy to assist with reservations. This is an operation that marries the old with the very modern and makes it work.

Burgundy House

6711 Washington Street
Yountville, California 94599; (707) 944-2855

INNKEEPERS:	*Bob and Mary Keenan.*
ACCOMMODATIONS:	*Six rooms and two cottages, five with shared bath. Twin and double beds.*
RESERVATIONS:	*Six to eight weeks for summer and weekends.*
MINIMUM STAY:	*None.*
DEPOSIT:	*First and last nights' lodging.*
CREDIT CARDS:	*AE, MC, VISA.*
RATES:	*Moderate to expensive.*
RESTRICTIONS:	*Children in cottages only. No pets.*

When Charles Rouvegneau constructed this amazingly sturdy house from local fieldstone (walls are twenty-two inches thick, posts and beams handcut) in the early 1870s, he used it as the center of his winery and brandy-distilling operations. And he built it just as if he were in the Saône of his native France. One of Charles's happiest inspirations was a huge hearth in which he baked bread daily to go with his best wine and brandy. Today you can eat breakfast by this same hearth, and there's no more snug or cozy nook in all the Napa Valley.

Each room is uniquely appointed with antiques, many from the countryside of France. But they're not necessarily just for looking at. Feel free to buy that lamp you like so much; everything is for sale! In fact, that's how Bob and Mary Keenan got into the innkeeping business. Friends shopping at their antique store were forever in need of a place to stay, and the store gradually evolved into an inn.

Surrounding the inn are roses and an herb garden. During the summer months the shaded patio in the back proves a favorite spot for those who come to dawdle. The village of Yountville hasn't grown much in population in the last hundred years, but it is a pleasant place in which to stroll any time of year. There was a bit too much chill in the air the night I visited, however, so I settled down in front of the crackling fire in the long, narrow common room downstairs.

No doubt about it: there's a French ambience here — nineteenth-century French at that. Burgundy House's sign contains a vignette of Napoleon III, a reminder of its French — or at least French-American — origins. It is one of the few older inns built exclusively of stone on this coast.

Later I relaxed in my room, pampered by silk sheets and a lush patterned comforter on my brass bed, enjoying the flower paintings on the wall and the decanted wine on the bureau. The moon was struggling to stay out, and in its cloudy light I could see Cabernet, Reisling, and Chardonnay vineyards from my window, as grey as the Grey Reisling I was drinking. Wine country, indeed!

Breakfast came early around a pine table in the hearth room below. Danish pastry, a fresh fruit platter (which sometimes includes strawberries in hollowed-out pineapples and stewed rhubarb in clear glass dishes), coffee, and my favorite, tangy fresh-squeezed OJ. It wasn't until I was ready to leave that I discovered two of the Keenans' most delightful secrets. One was their collection of antique games. The other was a remarkably *naïve* antique French birdcage.

There was another touch I particularly liked. No clocks. "Guests shouldn't have to worry about time," Mary avows firmly. *J'en veux plus!* Would that other inns would copy this. A most unusual and discerning place.

Bordeaux House

6600 Washington Street
Yountville, California 94599; (707) 944-2855

INNKEEPERS:	*Bob and Mary Keenan.*
ACCOMMODATIONS:	*Six rooms, all with private bath; twin and queen-size beds.*
RESERVATIONS:	*Two months for Saturday night.*
MINIMUM STAY:	*None.*
DEPOSIT:	*First and last nights' lodging.*
CREDIT CARDS:	*AE, MC, VISA.*
RATES:	*Moderate to expensive.*
RESTRICTIONS:	*No pets.*

If Burgundy House is the Keenans' *beau ideal* of the traditional French country inn transplanted to California, Bordeaux House is their *beau geste*, their no-holds-barred experiment with the ultra-modern. What a wildly contrasting pair of inns — both owned by the same couple! Bordeaux House is not only contemporary; its fine, clean brick lines are downright futuristic. Where Burgundy House lulls us with artfully recreated memories of things past, Bordeaux openly titil-lates us with visions of a California future. *Star Wars* creator George Lucas could do worse than to hire this couple if he ever needs an intergalactic b&b for his space fables.

Evocation of the future was exactly what architect Bob Keenan had in mind when he designed Bordeaux House. "I wanted something that would be a classic a hundred years from now, just like Burgundy House is today." All beds are on raised platforms (good for people with back trouble, incidentally); mirrors are ringed with soft makeup lights. The furniture is Italian contemporary.

The colors tend toward camel and burgundy. In my room the table was Plexiglas, as were the bathroom fixtures. Tailored fabrics are much in evidence; the lamps are mostly brass. Near my fireplace was a potted palm, a little triumph of audacity much in keeping with the rest of the tongue-in-cheek, yet decidedly relaxing decor.

Which is one of the effects the Keenans aimed to achieve. "We wanted rooms where a person can go and not be distracted by anything," Bob says. The aura of highly personalized simplicity present here is relaxing in ways the untrained eye may not always consciously perceive.

Daughter Jean is responsible for the wall graphics in the main living area. (Much of the original art here is her work.) The rooms have fresh flowers, a fireplace, a balcony, a private bath and patio, and a carafe of wine; the Keenans also put out lemon juice for those who are "thirsty after tasting wine all day."

Although coffee is served in the living area, guests go to Burgundy House for breakfast. The effect is magical. One slips out of the future and races straight back into the past without ever having passed Go. The two old Italian stone pines out in front add to the feeling of pleasant unreality.

A certain lightheartedness seems to cling to this inn, and is reflected in the kind of people who stay here. Mary recalls a party of ten who hid in a closet to surprise a birthday guest. Before you could say "Don Giovanni," the pranksters had gotten themselves locked in. And there they stayed — until the birthday friend arrived to let them out, much later than expected.

Throughout my stay here I kept searching for the one word that would best describe Bordeaux House. That word is *sophistication*. Thank you, Bob and Mary Keenan! If the future is anything like your fine inn, we haven't too much to worry about.

The Ink House

1575 St. Helena Highway
St. Helena, California 94574; (707) 963-3890

INNKEEPER:	*Lois Clark.*
ACCOMMODATIONS:	*Four rooms, all with private bath; double and queen-size beds.*
RESERVATIONS:	*Two weeks recommended.*
MINIMUM STAY:	*Two nights on weekends.*
DEPOSIT:	*Full amount.*
CREDIT CARDS:	*Not accepted.*
RATES:	*Moderate.*
RESTRICTIONS:	*No children under 12. No pets.*

T heron H. Ink, who built this huge and decidedly Italianate Victorian, operated not one but several vineyards, as well as ranches and a livery stable. He was a landholder in Marin, Sonoma, and Napa counties, serving as a Napa County supervisor for many years.

Ink House is still very much a private residence. (Guests use the parlor and dining room and lounge on the wide, wrap-around porch.) Proprietor Lois Clark and her husband George raised five children here, and it was when the children had left the nest that the bed and breakfast idea took hold. It's not hard to see why: Theron H. built this square, brown, white-trimmed residence on a palatial scale. Double stairways made it possible to divide the house in halves, one of which is for guests and the other for the Clarks.

There is no sign outside. (Lois doesn't want people who come just to gawk.) Once inside it took me some time to get used to the scale. (Ceilings are twelve feet high.) In the parlor I discovered a huge antique pump organ. In the bedrooms are more antiques, and handmade quilts.

My room was pink, with a brass-trimmed iron bed, white lace curtains, pink towels, and flowered wallpaper. The only truly modern touch here was the electric blanket — one that I genuinely appreciated.

Clever Lois keeps a book in which visitors are encouraged to review local restaurants, the better to inform you of which eateries are currently in favor. Lois's own Continental breakfast (served at 8:30) consists of juice, coffee, nut bread, and fruit. The bread is baked by Lois — she got in the habit of baking her own bread while she was raising her children.

Lois's most amusing moment as an innkeeper came the morning after Halloween when three young couples left a stuffed, three-armed monster at the breakfast table for her to find. She is a believer in intuition where guests are concerned. "You get a feeling for people — some want to talk, and some want to be left alone."

The Ink House is a place apart, a fascinating and very pleasant curiosity. What makes it interesting is its bold combination of styles. Its monumental scale seems to promise a kind of anonymity, yet what it ultimately delivers is a warm intimacy. The Ink House is finally a home, not a palace — but then Lois Clark could have told you that.

The White Ranch

707 White Lane
St. Helena, California 94574; (707) 963-4635

INNKEEPER:	*Ruth Davis.*
ACCOMMODATIONS:	*One room with private bath.*
RESERVATIONS:	*Two months recommended.*
MINIMUM STAY:	*None.*
DEPOSIT:	*First night's lodging.*
CREDIT CARDS:	*Not accepted.*
RATES:	*Moderate.*
RESTRICTIONS:	*No children. No pets.*

T alk about individual attention! You'll get it here for sure, because this delightful bed and breakfast caters to just one person (or couple) at a time. There is a private entrance to the bedroom; and although there may be only one (or two) of you, proprietor Ruth Davis maintains a dressing room and a private bath for the comfort of her visitors.

This lovely farm dwelling was built in 1865 by Asa White, a pioneer Methodist minister. (He arrived with his family in a covered wagon.) This is deep country: you are far enough from the highway not to hear traffic sounds. You *might* hear the sound of roosters cheerfully crowing you awake of a morning, and there are plenty of other farm animals to keep you company. (There are horses pastured here, and turkeys inhabit the barn.) Ancient walnut trees in the front yard complete the bucolic scene.

Ruth's accommodations are really closer to a certain kind of European-style bed and breakfast experience than many of the others toured. (In Europe and the British Isles a bed and breakfast establishment is just as likely to be somebody's home with a spare room as an inn.) One of the objectives of this arrangement is to cut down on the expense of hotels; but it also allows the guests to find out how the people of an area or region live and think. There's no better way to get close to people than to live in their home.

Ruth embarked on her bed and breakfasting adventure when her friend Lois Clark at the Ink House called to say she had a honeymoon couple—and no room at the inn, as it were. Ruth obliged by taking them in, and she's been at it ever since.

Anyone who's ever spent time on a farm will love her porch swing. There's a picnic table on the lawn; the parlor has a fireplace and a fine Queen Anne table and chairs. The guest room is furnished with heirlooms of Ruth's family. (Her grandmother's crocheted quilt is on the bed.) I liked the oversize mirror on the dressing table, too.

There is a small porch off the bedroom with a wooden bench for those who wish to sit and drink in the country silence. But I went to bed early, and my sleep was bone-deep and satisfying. When I woke up, refreshed and ravenous, Ruth presented me with homemade nut bread, popovers, orange juice, fresh fruit, and espresso. Delicious!

Traffic, job, crime, and noise pollution got you down? I recommend the White Ranch as the perfect antidote for your city blues.

Chalet Bernensis

225 St. Helena Highway
St. Helena, California 94574; (707) 963-4423

INNKEEPERS:	*Jack and Essie Doty.*
ACCOMMODATIONS:	*Fourteen rooms, nine with private bath; twin, double, and queen-size beds.*
RESERVATIONS:	*Three months recommended.*
MINIMUM STAY:	*Two nights on weekends.*
DEPOSIT:	*First night's lodging.*
CREDIT CARDS:	*MC, VISA.*
RATES:	*Moderate.*
RESTRICTIONS:	*No children under sixteen. No pets.*

St. Helena is indisputably one of the prettiest towns in the Napa Valley. And Chalet Bernensis is one of the nicest inns you'll find here, or anywhere else. Built in 1884 by John Thomann — he operated the Sutter Home Winery next door — it has been lovingly restored by Jack and Essie Doty. The original water tower (a common sight in the California countryside) has been carefully replicated and four of the inn's fourteen rooms are here. An additional five are found in the recently erected carriage house.

The Sutter Home Winery is still in operation. Just a few steps away, it seems a perfect place to begin one's wine-tasting activities. (Or festivities, as the case may be.) Other wineries within walking distance are Louis Martini, Sattui, and Heitz. Prestigious Inglenook and Christian Brothers are only a few miles away.

Chalet Bernensis is still very much a mansion — or rather an estate, as nineteenth-century vintners were fond of calling their winemaking fiefdoms. The grounds are spacious, with a long curved driveway. Gables are much in evidence. It is easy to imagine high-prancing horses and many-fringed surreys arriving with wealthy guests, as servants pour glasses of estate-bottled bubbly. Today guests arrive in a different kind of carriage, but the Victorian opulence lingers on.

All the rooms have antiques. Some bathrooms have claw-foot tubs and pedestal sinks, and many have fireplaces. I found my bed one of the most comfortable i had slept in on my tour. (My somnolence was enhanced by the presence of a lovely handmade quilt.) Breakfast was served between 8:30 and 10:00 A.M.: homemade scones (or muffins), fresh fruit, juices, and homemade jams and jellies, coffee and tea.

Although the Dotys have menus of all nearby restaurants on hand, you may wish to picnic on one of the picnic tables on the grounds. Or you might want to take in the Silverado museum, or enjoy the Calistoga hot springs. Touring has always been a part of this house; old photos from the 1880s demonstrate clearly that trolleys and trains came almost up to John Thomann's front door, loaded with the affluent and not-so-affluent on their way to Calistoga and its reputedly miraculous mineral waters.

Early wine merchants like John Thomann were classic bourgeois in the best sense. Like the medieval Florentines and the seventeenth-century Dutch, their nineteenth-century world was unapologetically elegant, yet essentially practical; homes were beautiful, but also the center of businesses, and of family life. Chalet Bernensis is a window onto that refined yet industrious sensibility that influenced California so much then — and still does.

Chestelson House

1417 Kearney Street
St. Helena, California 94574; (707) 963-2238

INNKEEPER:	*Claudia Chestelson.*
ACCOMMODATIONS:	*Two rooms, both with private bath; queen and king-size beds.*
RESERVATIONS:	*Three to four weeks.*
MINIMUM STAY:	*None.*
DEPOSIT:	*Full amount.*
CREDIT CARDS:	*Not accepted.*
RATES:	*Expensive.*
RESTRICTIONS:	*No children. No pets.*

T his understated but instantly intriguing Victorian may not have a past, or then again it may. Proprietor Claudia Chestelson awaits the definitive historian to sort out the welter of conflicting legends and hearsay that surround her home. But Chestelson House really doesn't need a past to capture the imagination. It has the vivacious, endlessly energetic Ms. Chestelson — and she's enough to relax and entertain even the most hard-pressed of workaholics.

She has given much thought to her bed and breakfast philosophy. "When you take people into your home, you are really doing something rather intimate — you are dealing with the most intimate aspects of people's lives." She pauses, and continues: "What you offer them — along with the intimacy — is a kind of elegance." She shrugs and laughs. "Nursemaid, psychologist, decorator — just say I offer free decorating tips and advice to the lovelorn."

Along with her unfailing taste and *joie de vivre*, Claudia also offers sherry in the rooms and is always happy to help with winery and restaurant reservations. My room was the front guest room. Definitely part of a home — but what attention to detail! A French armoire, a bay window with white shutters, a queen-size bed with a white comforter, a brass bedstead, an oval mirror with a wood frame — and fresh flowers, of course. (The bath is private but separate.)

Breakfast was pineapple with strawberries, pastries from the Court of Two Sisters bakery, French coffee with a touch of cinnamon, or tea. It arrived at the good, leisurely hour of 9:00 A.M. in the country kitchen (breakfast is also available in the main sitting room).

But watch out if you are single. Claudia loves bringing people together. One Marin County couple fell in love here and decided to get married; they spent their wedding night at Chestelson House. (And came back to celebrate their first anniversary.)

There is a fine view of St. Helena's surrounding hills. And St. Helena remains a permanent fascination for those who like to explore the picturesque and out of the way. The restaurants (Miramonte, Auberge du Soleil, French Laundry) are expensive but justly famous. And if you just like to sit with coffee or sherry on the wraparound veranda, you'll find that as pleasant as any of the local attractions.

Claudia Chestelson likes to give her guests personal attention, and it is her prodigious talent for pampering that makes the hours spent in her home such a memorable —and joyful — experience.

The Cinnamon Bear

1407 Kearney Street
St. Helena, California 94574; (707) 963-4653

INNKEEPER:	*Genny Jenkins.*
ACCOMMODATIONS:	*Three rooms, all with private bath; queen-size beds.*
RESERVATIONS:	*Two to four weeks.*
MINIMUM STAY:	*None.*
DEPOSIT:	*Full amount.*
CREDIT CARDS:	*AE, MC, VISA.*
RATES:	*Moderate.*
RESTRICTIONS:	*No children. No pets.*

T his lovely California bungalow was built in 1904 as a wedding present to Susan Smith Metzner from her father. Husband Walter Metzner was mayor of St. Helena for twenty years, and he lived with Susan in their comfortable home at 1407 Kearney Street until 1970. The present owner and creator of the Cinnamon Bear, Genny Jenkins, purchased the house in 1971 to provide a home for three growing children.

The bed and breakfast idea developed when oldest son David went to England and came back with enthusiastic reports of bed and breakfasts abroad. "So when the kids went to college," Genny says jokingly, "I changed the locks and rented out their rooms."

There was more to it than that, of course. It took tasteful, systematic remodeling of each room to provide the necessary facilities while giving each room its own character. The house had much character to begin with: broad wraparound porches — used for breakfast and general socializing in earlier days, as today — handcrafted redwood paneling, and a sitting room as well as a dining room all testify to the quality of life of its previous owners.

Mirrored built-ins, redwood beam ceilings, and ample bay windows covered by delicate lace curtains add to the homey elegance. The day I visited, there was a cheerful fire in the fireplace, plenty of sherry, games, and good books, and — a most important staple of the bed and breakfast trade — rocking chairs.

My room was similarly redolent of both taste and comfort: Persian rugs in tones of blue and burgundy. A white and burgundy comforter and pillow shams. A beige and brown private bath with a special country feeling. And, of course, bears: they are present in all sizes and variations throughout the house, although Genny is careful not to overdo the motif.

Breakfast (homemade breads, fresh fruit, coffee freshly ground in an antique coffee mill, and orange juice) is served in either the large dining room or on the porch (weather permitting). A nice touch of Americana: if the aroma of delicious food and fresh-brewed coffee doesn't waken you, the school bell next door will.

Genny likes to tell of the time she booked a couple over the phone and was then unexpectedly detained downtown. "The husband literally took over. When I got home a fire was lit, additional reservations had been made, wine poured, cheese served, and messages taken. Not only that — when I finally got back, he assumed I was a guest and proceeded to show me to my room." And where did the couple sleep? "In the basement — he'd booked all the available rooms!"

Friendly and *welcome* are two words that describe the Cinnamon Bear, a bed and breakfast that owes much of its appeal to the house — but most of it to the warm and enterprising woman who makes it a home.

Bale Mill Inn

3431 North St. Helena Highway
St. Helena, California 94574; (707) 963-4545

INNKEEPER:	*Tom Scheibal.*
ACCOMMODATIONS:	*Five rooms, three with private bath; double beds.*
RESERVATIONS:	*Three weeks.*
MINIMUM STAY:	*None.*
DEPOSIT:	*Full amount.*
CREDIT CARDS:	*MC, VISA.*
RATES:	*Inexpensive to moderate.*
RESTRICTIONS:	*No children under six. No pets.*

T he Bale Mill is a literary inn — and a place with a considerable sense of humor. Rooms are named and decorated after American literary figures. But don't let the reasonable prices and my descriptions of the whimsey and easy elegance here fool you; this is a very classy operation. Although proprietor Tom Scheibal has been in business only a short time, his establishment has already been chosen as the top country inn in the Napa Valley by Macy's, which featured it extensively in an advertising campaign built around a Wine Country inn theme.

Emily Dickinson's room is decorated like the porch of a New England country home — bravo, Tom! (Her room contains original wicker pieces and a love seat — a poignant choice, considering her lifelong self-isolation from the bustling New England world outside her shuttered windows.) Jack London (whose home was only a few miles away in Glen Ellen) is recalled by souvenirs of various heroic adventures, Indian relics, hilariously campy furniture — and a wolf under the bed.

Teddy Roosevelt is honored by crossed flags and antiques from his period. (There is a bugle on which a guest once played a muffled "charge" in the middle of the night.) The Captain Quinn room is the cabin of an imaginary character of nineteenth-century adventure-before-the-mast fiction of Robert Louis Stevenson and Melville.

(And created, one suspects, for the delight of Tom's young son, Quinn.) All rooms have a private deck and patio.

My favorite is the Hemingway room. It replicates a hotel room in Papa's beloved Key West (the ceiling fan revolves at a snail's pace; the floor is limed), but it is also a repository of effects and memorabilia that reflect the writer's career — and preoccupations (war canteen, safari helmet, mounted bull's horns). A hula dancer lamp, a potted palm, and shutters on the windows further suggest his Caribbean haunts and adventures.

Tom considers the Napa Valley healthier for his son than the city (the inn's environs include the historic bale mill after which the inn is named, a state park, moped rentals, golf, tennis, horseback riding and swimming). Breakfast at Bale Mill is certainly healthy: Tom's home-made cinnamon bread, pastries, fresh fruit, fresh-squeezed orange juice, and coffee. With rooms furnished with antiques from the time periods of famous American authors, what more could a tired and hungry writer like myself possibly want?

This is a reasonably priced and extremely original bed and breakfast experience that even nonwriters shouldn't miss. Go now, before the mobs arrive — as they surely will.

Larkmead Country Inn

1103 Larkmead Lane
Calistoga, California 94515; (707) 942-5360

INNKEEPERS:	*Gene and Joan Garbarino.*
ACCOMMODATIONS:	*Four rooms, all with private bath; double and twin beds.*
RESERVATIONS:	*Four to five weeks for weekends.*
MINIMUM STAY:	*None.*
DEPOSIT:	*First night's lodging.*
CREDIT CARDS:	*Not accepted.*
RATES:	*Expensive.*
RESTRICTIONS:	*No children. No pets.*

G ene and Joan Garbarino don't have a sign out front, and they don't advertise their inn — they don't have to. Most of their bookings are repeat business and the rest come by word of mouth. People who like this place tend to like it very much; it's not hard to see why. Classical yet simple, in a tranquil setting literally in the heart of a vineyard, perhaps the best word to describe Larkmead Country Inn is *serene.*

This inn on old Larkmead Lane is located next to famed Hanns Kornell Champagne Cellars; it was built by the son of an earlier vintner, on the occasion of his marriage. The house abounds with antiques, paintings, and prints from the Garbarinos' collection; Persian carpets, broad porches, wide clapboards, and a certain atmosphere of unperturbable solidity all suggest a New England inn. Until one looks out the window, that is: all rooms overlook row on row of vineyards.

It is not particularly surprising, then, that all rooms are named after wines of the Napa Valley. The Beaujolais has an antique sewing machine and a private porch from which you see all the way to the hills on the edge of the valley on a clear and moonlit night. The Chardonnay Room features antique brass twin beds, white wicker chairs, red and white flowered spreads — and the fresh flowers and complimentary decanter of wine that all guests receive.

It so happens that my favorite room here is also my favorite wine. The elegant Chenin Blanc Room has a chaise lounge I loved, curtains and matching wallpaper, an armoire, a white wicker chair and table — and a very comfy double bed. The living room is comfortable, too — Joan's afternoon tea was especially pleasant in front of a blazing fire in the fireplace. The Garbarinos have chess, cards, puzzles, dominoes, and many books on hand to occupy the idle hand and mind.

Breakfast is served on one of the porches, when weather permits; mine arrived in the dining room. (And it arrived on fine china with sterling silver and linen napkins, I might add.) It consisted of fresh fruit, freshly ground coffee, and a basket of croissants, scones, and French rolls with sweet butter and homemade preserves.

The Garbarinos are from Orinda; Gene is a dentist. Both feel that their part of the Napa Valley is especially beautiful at harvest time. And both are happy to be serving the public in such a direct and personal way. "When's the last time you heard of a hotel receiving a thank-you note?" Joan asks. She adds with a touch of awe: "I've received twenty-three!"

That's as good an indication as any I've heard of the difference between a hotel and the bed and breakfast experience.

Wine Way Inn

1019 Foothill Boulevard, Highway 29
Calistoga, California 94515; (707) 942-0680

INNKEEPERS:	*Allen and Dede Good.*
ACCOMMODATIONS:	*Four rooms, two with private bath; twin, double, and queen-size beds.*
RESERVATIONS:	*Four weeks recommended for weekends in April and November.*
MINIMUM STAY:	*Two nights.*
DEPOSIT:	*Full amount.*
CREDIT CARDS:	*MC, VISA.*
RATES:	*Moderate.*
RESTRICTIONS:	*No children. No pets.*

A llen and Dede Good had always wanted to work together in a joint venture, and Dede had stayed at bed and breakfasts in Europe. While vacationing in Napa Valley in 1980, they talked to a realtor. Only a few short months later, they had relocated from Los Angeles and opened their doors to the bed and breakfast public. Both are vigorous proponents of the owner-operated school of innkeeping.
he manages an auto body shop) but both are vigorous proponents of the owner-operated school of innkeeping.

Their house, built in 1915 as a family home, has many of the characteristics of a country house: the Mayacamas Mountains come right down to meet the redwood deck in back. Rooms are named after towns on Highway 29, the main wine country route. St. Helena — the room where I slept, and my favorite — has a bed fit for a queen (and in fact is queen size), a private bath, an armoire, and — an especially nice touch — a basket of colored yarn compatible with the patchwork quilt on the bed. (Dede later told me it came from her home in Indiana.) There was also a candle and candlestick, a piece which more inns should consider placing in their rooms for those of us who find candlelight relaxing just before bedtime.

The comfortable living room sports a cozy fireplace, English china and pottery, an antique clock on the mantel, and (the day I was there) a decanter of excellent Inglenook Chablis. For those who enjoy excursions, Dede is happy to prepare a "hobo picnic": everything but wine for guests to take on their winery tours (including a picnic cloth for the table).

This poised and attractive couple get around to local restaurants, and are glad to share first-hand impressions. "We conduct a service for travelers in the area," Dede says, "and if they want help finding their way around, we provide it." Both she and her husband are quick to add that if the guest's first priority is privacy, that preference is strictly observed.

Local attractions include the Sharpsteen Museum (memorabilia, antiques, and photographs of Calistoga from its glory days as a flourishing resort of the 1860s) and a petrified forest. Why not try a mud bath? It's inexpensive and relaxing, and an experience you won't soon forget. (Just don't let friends take pictures, or you may never hear the end of it.)

Breakfast at Wine Way is Continental: fruit of the season, freshly squeezed orange juice, homemade cakes and pastries, tea, and coffee.

Culver's, A Country Inn

1805 Foothill Blvd.
Calistoga, California 94515; (707) 942-4535

INNKEEPERS:	*George Hunt and Philip Eyre.*
ACCOMMODATIONS:	*Seven rooms share three baths; twin, double, queen- and king-size beds.*
RESERVATIONS:	*Four to six weeks recommended.*
MINIMUM STAY:	*Two nights on weekends.*
DEPOSIT:	*First night's lodging.*
CREDIT CARDS:	*MC, VISA.*
RATES:	*Moderate.*
RESTRICTIONS:	*No children under twelve. No pets.*

S am Brannan is credited with many California "firsts": he was the state's first millionaire, banker, and land developer, and he published San Francisco's first newspaper, the *California Star*. It was, in fact, a notice in Brannan's publication that drew the outside world's attention to the discovery of gold at Sutter's Mill in 1848 — and the rush was on.

In the early 1860s, Brannan secured a parcel of land at the northernmost edge of what is now the renowned Napa Valley. In an attempt to persuade investors to assist him develop it into a summer resort patterned after Saratoga, New York, he held a lavish dinner party. His guests were transported by boat from San Francisco to Vallejo, and by train from Vallejo to the site he had selected in the foothills of Mount St. Helena. The champagne flowed freely, and as legend has it when Sam stood up to make his formal proposal he remarked: "We'll make this the Calistoga of Sarafornia!"

Brannan died in 1889, but the village he founded, Calistoga, continues to this day as a resort with numerous spas, mud baths, and mineral hot springs.

An enduring historical landmark of this same genre is Culver's, a country inn located on Calistoga's Foothill Boulevard just north of Highway 29. This early 1870s

Victorian was built by Maj. John Oscar Culver, a Milwaukee newspaperman who headed west for reasons unknown. The house is carefully appointed with antiques of the period and with uniquely designed quilts. Let it not be said, however, that Culver's is without its modern conveniences. The inn boasts showers, air conditioning, a sauna, a spa, and a swimming pool.

Menus from local restaurants are available, as are guidebooks on the Napa Valley. Additional reading material includes *National Geographic, Time,* and *Smithsonian* magazines, as well as best-selling paperbacks. Games are found on the rolltop desk in the breakfast room. A decanter of cream sherry sits in the living room next to the player piano.

Homemade scones and sour cream coffee cake are part of the sit-down breakfast with its fresh-fruit starter, served from 8:30 to 10:00.

The innkeepers are not numbered among the list of main attractions here, nor do they care to be. Their objective is to provide a setting where one can reflect on people like Sam Brannan, who shaped and enlivened the history of California — and engage in the activities that enrich the Californians of today.

WHITEGATE INN

The
MENDOCINO
COAST

Westport

Cobweb Palace

Howard Creek Ranch

Blue Rose Inn
Country Inn
Glass Beach Inn
Grey Whale Inn
Pudding Creek Inn

Fort Bragg

Headlands Inn
Joshua Grindle Inn

Mendocino

Whitegate Inn

Little River

Glendeven
Victorian Farmhouse

Albion

128

101

Ukiah

Elk

Elk Cove Inn
Green Dolphin Inn

128

1

Old Milano Hotel
St. Orres
Whale Watch Inn

Gualala

Cloverdale

Old Milano Hotel

38300 Highway One
Gualala, California 95445; (707) 884-3256

INNKEEPERS:	*Colette Tessier and Leslie Linscheid.*
ACCOMMODATIONS:	*Nine rooms, three with private bath; double and queen-size beds.*
RESERVATIONS:	*Four weeks recommended.*
MINIMUM STAY:	*Two nights on weekends.*
DEPOSIT:	*First night's lodging.*
CREDIT CARDS:	*AE, MC, VISA.*
RATES:	*Moderate to expensive.*
RESTRICTIONS:	*No children. No pets.*

I n 1905 Bert Luccinetti built a restaurant and pub on a cliff overhanging Castle Rock, alongside what was then a busy railroad and stage road. (It catered mainly to lumbermen.) New owners made it into a resort for fishermen in the 1920s; the 1950s saw it modernized, its Victorian heritage obscured by various layers of ticky-tacky "improvements." Today it is one of the most highly regarded inns on the northern California coast, thanks to the efforts of Colette Tessier and Leslie Linscheid, both former Macy's employees who put their business and buying skills to work in this impressive blend of old and new (now recorded in the National Register of Historical Places).

The inn has seven rooms and two cottages — one a caboose where the old railroad once ran. It has walls of sandblasted wood, a galley, and a red pot-bellied stove. Two brakemen's seats for taking in the sunsets can be reached by a ladder.

Beds, bureaus, tables, lampshades, quilts, and bric-a-brac have been chosen with loving care. Morris wallpapers, original paintings, redwood wainscoting in the halls, and old-fashioned car-sided ceilings are also featured. A canopy bed highlights the Master Suite where the Luccinetti family lived. You will also see Eastlake chairs, Tiffany lamps galore, and a sofa that was the first Riviera bed made in 1906.

The gracious Wine Parlor is made cheerful by a great stone fireplace. Adjacent are the quieter and more reflective comforts of the Music Room; *aficionados* of art books will find a fine collection. The staff of the Old Milano will arrange for you to have a massage by a certified massage practitioner, according to its brochure. Another of the more comfortable concessions to modern sensibilities is a hot tub facing the ocean. (It is encircled by an old-fashioned knob-topped fence for privacy.)

Room No. 4, with its breathtaking ocean view, was my favorite. The wallpaper design is in shades of blue, lilac, pink, and green. There's a comfortable overstuffed rocker facing the tumultuous Pacific. An oval wood-framed mirror and fresh flowers in a pitcher complete the feeling of restful privacy.

Breakfast consists of unique homemade breads (Ukrainian poppy seed cake and banana coconut) with sweet butter, yogurt, and locally roasted coffee and tea. Guests may have their breakfast on the loggia, in the gardens, or in their room.

I left the Old Milano revitalized. Its setting is sensational, but the main ingredient of its success is the taste of its owners. There is something dreamlike in its unique compound of the Victorian and the modern. The Old Milano is like an image from art made real, and its restfulness is to a large extent due to its ability to make us feel that we are a part of another, more ordered world.

St. Orres

36601 Highway One South, P.O. Box 523
Gualala, California 95445; (707) 884-3303

INNKEEPERS:	*Ted Black, Rich Wasserman, Eric Black, Rosemary Campiformio.*
ACCOMMODATIONS:	*Eight rooms and three cottages, three rooms with private bath; double and queen-size beds.*
RESERVATIONS:	*Three months for weekends.*
MINIMUM STAY:	*Two nights in cottages and ocean-view rooms on the weekends.*
DEPOSIT:	*Full amount.*
CREDIT CARDS:	*MC, VISA.*
RATES:	*Moderate to expensive.*
RESTRICTIONS:	*Children in cottages only. No pets.*

T he windswept isolation and wild charm of this part of the Mendocino coast is staggering. The environs (not to mention the elements) seem to demand one of two architectural styles: rigorous simplicity or the same spendthrift abandon that nature has lavished on her handiwork in the area. Master craftsman Eric Black opted for the latter. The result is a fantasy, an explosion of fine art, an architectural wonder.

It was just a few years ago that he and carpenter Richard Wasserman bought the remains of the old Seaside Hotel (built in the 1920s) and went to work on it. Oregon red cedar was used to transform the exterior, topped off by twin domed towers, deliberately reminiscent of the homeland of the Russian trappers who settled the area. Is it any wonder that passersby stop to marvel at this audacious Russophilic beauty in the wilderness?

The fairy-tale extravagance continues inside. The entrance hall has some very fine Art Nouveau and Edwardian pieces, and highly detailed stained-glass windows. The sitting room is dominated by a castle-size fireplace that looks like it belongs in Charles Laughton's

Henry the Eighth banquet scene. (And *six* oak doors, with stained-glass windows in each.) The dining room rises a dizzying three stories to an octagonal dome above, with row on row of windows culminating in a single rank of stained-glass panes just below its copper-domed crown.

The two front rooms have direct ocean views and French doors that open onto a balcony. Most rooms share baths "down the hall" — a His, a Hers, and a spacious Ours with tiled tub enclosures and dual shower heads. Quilts by Gualala quilt maker Donna Bishop are lush velvet; rooms have intricate redwood paneling. (Even the telephone is paneled in redwood.)

The newest accommodation is the Tree House. This experiment in luxury contains a lovely queen-size brass bed, a tile bath with a deep sunken tub, a carpet, and its own kitchenette. As if that weren't enough, there is a Franklin stove fireplace with a hand-painted tile hearth; the living room has an ocean view, with French doors leading onto a sun deck.

Other than Rosemary Campiformio's long standing enjoyment in serving people, none of the four friends (Ted Black is Eric's uncle) had any inn or restaurant experience when they began. This has not handicapped them. Their restaurant has already achieved a considerable reputation. The complimentary breakfast is served from 8:30 to 9:30 and consists of homemade pastries, yogurt with nuts and raisins, homemade granola, and fresh-fruit juices.

For me the words that best describe St. Orres are *magic* and *extravagance.* And perhaps the most wonderful part of it are the genuinely reasonable prices.

Whale Watch Inn

35100 Highway One
Gualala, California 95445; (707) 884-3667

INNKEEPERS:	*Irene and Enoch Stewart.*
ACCOMMODATIONS:	*Six rooms, all with private bath; queen-size beds.*
RESERVATIONS:	*Three to four weeks recommended.*
MINIMUM STAY:	*Two nights on weekends.*
DEPOSIT:	*First night's lodging.*
CREDIT CARDS:	*AE, MC, VISA.*
RATES:	*Moderate to expensive.*
RESTRICTIONS:	*No children. No pets.*

Whale Watch Inn wasn't planned, it just "happened," according to Enoch and Irene Stewart, who purchased the two-acre property overlooking Anchor Bay and the south Mendocino coastline in 1970. Enoch, then president of an architectural design firm, built Whale Watch (a hexagonal-shaped dwelling with floor-to-ceiling windows on three sides, a central fireplace, and a magnificent view of the ever-changing Pacific) for use as the family's second home. In 1976 the Stewarts constructed a four-room "addition," and October 1978 saw the official opening of the Whale Watch Inn.

The buildings' contemporary architecture has incorporated spacious decks, skylights, and natural-wood interiors. Some of the rooms have fireplaces, others have private spas, four include fully equipped kitchens, and all are supplied with magazines, books, candles, wineglasses, mints, and beach towels.

The Golden Voyage Suite's contemporary furnishings and freestanding Swedish fireplace are framed by the room's many angles and high, beamed ceiling; its cinnamon carpet blends nicely with the redwood walls. The Provence Room's spiral staircase leads to a sitting room where furnishings follow a French country motif. The queen-size bed features a lovely walnut and cane headboard with a matching chest; a chaise longue, upholstered in a wisteria and teal print, picks up the teal in the carpet and the colorful bedspread. The room also has a fireplace, a wet bar, and a window seat. There's a two-person whirlpool spa in the bath that allows you to soak in the tub and look out to sea at the same time, and the deck features yet another fantastic view of the ocean, framed by cypress trees.

Guests of the Whale Watch dine in the Whale Watch room, hub of the inn's activities, or on the deck, weather permitting. Guests of the "addition" receive their breakfast in a decorative basket. A fresh-fruit compote (strawberries, grapes, melon, bananas, and peaches in season) flavored with coconut and Triple Sec is accompanied with creamy vanilla yogurt (or Brie), scones, and hot lemon bread, as well as locally blended coffee and tea.

Whale Watch is located at the northern edge of Anchor Bay, a protected inlet with white sandy beaches and calm waters for diving, boating, and swimming. The site's "banana belt" weather affords an escape from the usual coastal fog. Sea lions and pelicans (as well as whales) can be seen from both beach and cliff side.

Elk Cove Inn

6300 South Highway One
Elk, California 95432; (707) 877-3321

INNKEEPER:	Hildrun-Uta Triebess.
ACCOMMODATIONS:	Nine rooms, seven with private bath; double and queen-size beds.
RESERVATIONS:	Two weeks recommended for weekends.
MINIMUM STAY:	None.
DEPOSIT:	$50 to $100.
CREDIT CARDS:	Not accepted.
RATES:	Moderate to expensive.
RESTRICTIONS:	No children under eight. No pets.

This sweet Victorian was built in the early 1890s by the L.E. White Lumber Company. (L.E. built it for his son, who was the superintendent of his mill.) From 1890 to the crash in 1929 the nearby hamlet of Elk was a booming lumber port. Now it is the quintessential sleepy coast village. And this small but charming bed and breakfast inn is the archetypical Mendocino bed and breakfast — provided you come here to get away from everything. Because there is nothing — literally *nothing* — to do here but walk, read, eat, and sleep. If it is a period of total rest you are looking for, this is definitely the place for you.

Hildrun was born in Germany but was brought to this country early in life; she is a skilled cook, specializing in European cookery (dinner is served here on weekends as well as breakfast). Friendly, cosmopolitan, and very amusing, this Hildrun, whose talent for entertaining is a central attraction of her operation.

"What I strive for is giving people things they don't do for themselves at home," Hildrun says, "yet in a way that makes them *feel* like they are at home." Which is, by the way, perhaps the best formula for a successful bed and breakfast; it gives the guest a refuge from the cares and problems of home — while at the same time replicating (or at least simulating) a feeling of "at-homeness."

There are two parts, or phases, to Elk Cove Inn. One is the main house, where Hildrun lives. Here are two guest rooms; guests sit in the evening by the fire to hear her extensive collection of classical music. Most guests find themselves in Sandpiper House, an annex originally built for visitors to the lumber company. It is about half a mile away.

Sandpiper House is flanked by handsome camellia trees. There is a large redwood-paneled common room, again with a brick fireplace. My favorite room is No. 2, featuring a view of the ocean that took my breath away. (The old-fashioned flowered-wallpaper design and slightly campy potted palm were just right for this room.) Paths lead from both houses to private, secluded beaches.

Breakfast here is a delight. Hildrun is well known for her German egg cakes (Eierkuchen) with freshly picked blackberries or huckleberries, coffee, and orange juice. For dinner you might be served Königsberger Klops (poached meatballs in lemon-caper sauce), Sauerbraten, Rouladen, Hasenpfeffer (rabbit in a sour cream sauce) — or any number of excellent French dishes.

Green Dolphin Inn

6145 South Highway One, P.O. Box 132
Elk, California 95432; (707) 877-3342

INNKEEPERS:	*Bill Reed and Elaine Beldin.*
ACCOMMODATIONS:	*Three rooms, all with private bath; two queen-size and one king-size bed.*
RESERVATIONS:	*Three weeks recommended.*
MINIMUM STAY:	*Two nights.*
DEPOSIT:	*First night's lodging.*
CREDIT CARDS:	*Not accepted.*
RATES:	*Moderate.*
RESTRICTIONS:	*No children. No pets.*

I liked this unpretentious, very comfortable bed and breakfast as much for the people who are the hosts as for the environment it provides. The cozy interiors are a delight, but the sincere and unaffected enthusiasm of proprietors Bill Reed and Elaine Beldin is the main attraction here. I'm apparently not the only person who feels this way; a solid majority of the guests at any time represents repeat business.

Bill Reed was a bookkeeper before he was an innkeeper; Elaine Beldin was a legislative secretary in Sacramento. When midlife crisis made its inevitable appearance, the two friends decided to confront it together. They had always liked this part of the California coastline, so when the chance presented itself, they took the plunge into the uncertain waters of the bed and breakfast business.

I'm glad they did. The heavily beamed, spacious Commons Room contains one of the most massive fireplaces I've seen. Books in the library lean heavily toward the classics; there are also games for those whose taste runs to less introspective amusements. But it was the cheerful warmth of Bill and Elaine that impressed me most. Their pride in their establishment was obvious as they showed me the rest of their accommodations.

The kitchen and dining room are on the second

floor, offering what Elaine unabashedly refers to as "a truly magnificent view." The dining room has a fireplace, and there is a small balcony directly adjacent to it. (There is also a small sitting area on the second floor.) The single bedroom on this level sports a very large and somewhat Gothic-looking wood stove. The other two bedrooms are in the Carriage House in back, with a deck and a hot tub nearby. All rooms contain antiques, many of which are for sale.

The thing for which the Green Dolphin is perhaps best known (besides the friendliness of its proprietors) is its hearty breakfast. The bill of fare changes regularly, but the one unalterable house rule is that no one goes away hungry. This very American all-you-can-eat policy contrasts markedly with the Continental breakfast. "People like to feel special," Elaine says, "and I simply enjoy making them feel that way."

Victorian Farmhouse

7001 North Highway One, P.O. Box 357
Little River, California 95456; (707) 937-0697

INNKEEPERS:	*Thomas and Jane Szilasi.*
ACCOMMODATIONS:	*Five rooms, all with private bath; queen- and king-size beds.*
RESERVATIONS:	*Three to four weeks recommended.*
MINIMUM STAY:	*Two nights on weekends.*
DEPOSIT:	*First night's lodging.*
CREDIT CARDS:	*Not accepted.*
RATES:	*Moderate.*
RESTRICTIONS:	*No children under sixteen. No pets.*

I t was built in 1877 by John and Emma Dora Dennen as a private residence, which it still is. A pronounced feeling of privacy is the most striking attribute of this homey inn. But a certain atmosphere of permanence — of stability — runs it a close second. One doesn't visit here so much as reside, even if the duration of that residence is only a week or a weekend.

Thomas Szilasi was once a pharmaceutical salesman; his wife Jane was a stewardess for TWA. They lived in the sprawling, ever-growing metropolis of San Jose. One day they sat down and wrote a list of all the things they liked, as well as the things they didn't. (A wise and provident couple, these two.) Bed and breakfast inns were close to the top of their list of likable things, so when this property became available they decided to settle down with an inn of their own.

Then came the hard work. Tom did the "nail-bending" part of the restoration; Jane was the master decorator. Both gloried in the lack of neon signs, stoplights, and billboards in Little River. "It's nice to get back to basics," says Tom. "I enjoy taking people at their word, trusting people." It's something that seems to happen more in the country than the city, they feel.

They also feel that their inn is ideal for traveling couples. There are several acres — and an orchard of apple, plum, and pear — to ramble around in. I liked the solid triple-hung bay windows in the downstairs parlor, the Regulator clock, and the fireplace. Both upstairs rooms have ocean views, while one downstairs has a French wood-burning stove and its own sitting room. (The other has an exquisite view of a small private flower garden.)

A queen-size brass bed graces the Emma Dora room; there are white comforters and pillow shams, and a ceiling done in a tasteful (and restful) redwood design. I also liked the upstairs sitting room with its view of the rear flower gardens.

Breakfast arrives promptly at 8:30 — guests are served in their rooms. (Bran and raisin muffins, peach yogurt with sliced bananas and granola, fresh OJ, and coffee, tea, or hot chocolate.) Other typical morning dishes are croissants, apple juice, and fresh fruit in season. Sometimes guests are served fruit fresh from the orchard outside.

Whatever you eat in the morning, the fresh ocean breeze in these parts will make it taste better than anything you could eat in the city. The quiet pace and restful environment of this inn is most conducive to concentration and creativity — an excellent place to sort out one's thoughts and prepare emotionally for that big project back in the workaday world.

Glendeven

8221 North Highway One
Little River, California 95456; (707) 937-0083

INNKEEPERS:	*Jan and Janet deVries.*
ACCOMMODATIONS:	*Ten rooms, eight with private bath; queen-size beds.*
RESERVATIONS:	*Three months for weekends; two weeks Monday through Thursday.*
MINIMUM STAY:	*Two nights on weekends.*
DEPOSIT:	*First night's lodging.*
CREDIT CARDS:	*By special arrangement.*
RATES:	*Moderate to expensive.*
RESTRICTIONS:	*No children under eight. No pets.*

G lendeven was the country home of Isaiah Stevens, who moved here with a group of settlers from Maine. He raised and bred fine horses and cattle on his one-hundred-acre farm — and also built a farmhouse in 1867 for his bride, Rebecca Coombs. It was and is a distinctly New England-looking house, typical of the architecture in the Mendocino area; many of the early settlers were from that region.

In the 1950s the house was bought by Warren and Dora Zimmer, who began its restoration. Jan deVries, who was then a student, saw it during a visit to the coast in 1962. He returned later as a teacher, and married Janet Bell — and the couple then left for Portland. But the rugged north coast (and perhaps the romance associated with their courtship) continued to exert its pull. When the deVries heard of the impending sale of the Zimmer house in 1977, they returned to buy and open it as an inn.

This is the perfect place to get over a bad case of office politics, a disappointment in love, or the kind of blahs associated with the morning headlines. The dominant note here is upbeat. Antique furnishings sit side by side with contemporary pieces, ceramics, and works of art; colorful, cheery abstract paintings hang on the walls. The effect is quite consciously calculated to elevate the mood. And it succeeds admirably.

My favorite rooms are the Garret, a surprisingly large attic room with skylights, tucked under the eaves of the roof (with a rocking chair and a writing desk); and the Garden Room with its French bedroom set, large hanging plants, and country-meadow atmosphere. Guests in both rooms are invited to breakfast on a tray or to come out and mingle with the other guests. The deVries say that breakfast is "somewhere in between" full and Continental: bread or muffins, coffee cake, hard-cooked eggs, juice, and a variety of fresh fruits — including, if you are lucky, their tasty baked apples.

Exploring the sitting room, I discovered a grand piano and a row of large-paned windows looking out on the grounds, which contain several bright gardens. The light and airy feeling was enhanced by the large original barn in back (which, now remodeled, is the innkeepers' home) and the lovely old cypress trees that flank and surround both structures.

Not far from Glendeven, a sense of the forest begins. But it is not Robert Frost's "lovely, dark, and deep" New England woods. Rather it is a place of laughter, a certain youthful playfulness, and the bright colors of an uncomplicated childhood. Again it is Frost who expresses this sense of childlike play: "So was I once a swinger of birches. And so I dream of going back to be."

Headlands Inn

44950 Albion Street
Mendocino, California 95460; (707) 937-4431

INNKEEPERS:	*Lynn Anderson, Pete Albrecht, and Kathy Casper.*
ACCOMMODATIONS:	*Five rooms and a cottage, all with private bath; queen and king-size beds.*
RESERVATIONS:	*Four weeks recommended.*
MINIMUM STAY:	*Two nights on weekends.*
DEPOSIT:	*First night's lodging.*
CREDIT CARDS:	*Not accepted.*
RATES:	*Moderate.*
RESTRICTIONS:	*No children. No pets.*

T he Headlands Inn began as a barbershop on Main Street in the town of Mendocino in 1868. Five years later a second story was added for the barber and his family. Afterwards the dwelling was used as a saloon, a hotel annex, and a private residence. In 1883 it was moved to its present location at Howard and Albion streets. Bessie Strauss and her husband John bought the house in 1924; renovation was completed in 1979.

The building was already an inn when Kathy Casper found that it was up for sale (she lived three miles up the road). At that time Peter Albrecht and Lynn Anderson were living in the Virgin Islands; they longed to settle in the Pacific Northwest. The three entrepreneurs got together and formed a partnership, and are now collectively the owner-operators of the Headlands.

The dwelling is three stories high, with clean, solid lines — most definitely a Victorian with a New England character. The modern conveniences are not lacking; all six rooms have private bathrooms, and all have fireplaces. Two are attic rooms with window seats, the best view of the town I saw while I was there. (Look particularly for Mendocino's quaint water tower.) One room comes with a private balcony.

My favorite room is No. 2: bay windows facing the

ocean, a redwood fireplace, a large mirrored armoire, a
rocking chair, lace curtains — and a wonderful king-size
bed truly fit for a king.

Breakfast is fresh-baked breads and muffins, freshly
squeezed orange juice or fresh fruit, coffee and tea. It
arrives on a breakfast tray with fresh flowers. (The day I
was there a delicious lemon bread was part of the morning menu.)

Local attractions are many and varied. There is an
art center, secluded sandy beaches, tide pools teeming
with marine life, hiking (three state parks are within ten
miles of Mendocino), golfing, and canoeing on Big
River. But for many, simply walking through Mendocino is enough: it bears an astonishing resemblance to a
New England fishing village and has been used as a back-
drop for Hollywood productions. There are many fine
restaurants in the area; complimentary wine is served in
the afternoon at the Headlands.

Joshua Grindle Inn

44800 Little Lake, P.O. Box 647
Mendocino, California 95460; (707) 937-4143

INNKEEPERS:	*Gwen and Bill Jacobson.*
ACCOMMODATIONS:	*Nine rooms, all with private bath; queen-size beds.*
RESERVATIONS:	*Ten to twelve weeks recommended.*
MINIMUM STAY:	*Two nights on weekends.*
DEPOSIT:	*First night's lodging.*
CREDIT CARDS:	*Not accepted.*
RATES:	*Moderate.*
RESTRICTIONS:	*Children discouraged. No pets.*

L ike so many others, the Grindle clan had come to the North Coast from Maine. This lovely Italianate home was built as a wedding present on the marriage of Joshua Grindle and Alice Hills, in 1879 — a gift from the bride's father. Alice died in childbirth in 1882, but the house remained in the Grindle family until 1967. In 1977 Bill and Gwen Jacobson bought the house and turned it into a first-class inn.

The Jacobsons have so enhanced the "back east" tone of this intricate bed and breakfast that it can stand up to the very best New England establishment. And it is a very romantic place; a natural, I would think, for a honeymoon.

The first things I noticed on entering were the Early American pieces in the parlor (along with the fireplace and grand piano). Colonial-era furnishings appear extensively throughout the rest of the house. (All guest rooms have handmade quilts from New England.) The Library Room has an old-fashioned four-poster and fine handcrafted cabinets and shelves. In the dining room I found a harvest table seating ten, and Pennsylvania Dutch-style wallpaper. Impeccable taste and cleanliness add to the eastern feeling.

In back there is a cottage with two rooms, a Franklin stove, wood-beamed ceilings, and a large bath. (Both rooms are accessible by wheelchair.) A recently constructed water tower houses two additional accommodations.

The Grindle has a good collection of old clocks that will remind you pleasantly of all the time you have to fritter away. I also liked the extensive collection of etchings, oil paintings, and serigraphs. Two of the guest rooms in the main house have fireplaces decorated with hand-crafted tiles done in 1870 at Ninton's, Stoke on Trent, a factory in England. (The tiles in the Library Room illustrate *Aesop's Fables*.)

Gwen serves an ample breakfast that includes eggs from a nearby farm, fresh fruit, coffee cake, huckleberry muffins, popovers, homemade bread, tea and coffee. There are always apples and oranges in the parlor for guests, as well as a decanter of sherry. And bicycles are available to guests for exploring this most interesting of little coastal enclaves.

Whitegate Inn

499 Howard Street, P.O. Box 150
Mendocino, California 95460; (707) 937-4892

INNKEEPERS:	*Robbie and Wally Clegg.*
ACCOMMODATIONS:	*Six rooms, four with private bath; twin, double, and queen-size beds. Fireplaces and ocean views.*
RESERVATIONS:	*Three to four weeks recommended.*
MINIMUM STAY:	*Two nights on weekends.*
DEPOSIT:	*First night's lodging.*
CREDIT CARDS:	*Not accepted.*
RATES:	*Moderate.*
RESTRICTIONS:	*Children discouraged. No pets.*

T his house was built in 1880 by Dr. William McCornack, a local physician. He used it as his hospital, and it retained its healing-arts association well into living memory; it was called the McCornack Healing Center before its purchase by Bill Reed and Elaine Beldin (now owners of the Green Dolphin Inn in Elk). Robbie and Wally Clegg finished the restoration begun by Bill and Elaine — exactly one hundred years after the inn was built.

Many things have changed in the last hundred years, but not the service orientation of the building's succession of owners. Robbie enjoys serving people; in fact, she feels people don't ask for enough. "It's as though they think they'll be *imposing* if they ask for something." Don't feel that way when you visit Whitegate. Your hosts will not only be two of the youngest innkeepers I have encountered (they are both in their early thirties), but among the most enthusiastic. Their innkeeping style includes spending as much time as possible with guests and acting as their guides through the north coast panorama.

Wally and Robbie lived in Marin County before moving to Mendocino. She worked as a bartender (now *there's* a serving profession for you!); Wally was in the computer business. Both had stayed at bed and breakfast inns in northern California and the Pacific Northwest. They heard about the McCornack house through Mendocino's real estate grapevine, and, after purchasing it, filled it with pieces once possessed by former owners, antiques with a local history, and a few special family heirlooms.

The house is well appointed, with gilt ceiling moldings and plaster medallions; the parlor contains two Victorian settees, a grand Hamilton pump organ, lots of green plants, a stereo system, and a good collection of local-interest books for those curious about the area. Breakfast is served in the parlor, as is wine in the afternoon.

The morning meal is a generous one. A full breakfast is served on the weekends (featuring excellent banana-nut waffles when I stayed here — the Cleggs are noted for the variety of waffles they serve); weekdays guests receive a Continental breakfast of nut breads with cream cheese and flavored butters, fresh fruit, coffee, and tea.

I slept in the Cypress Room: bay windows, a beautiful red-dragon design Oriental carpet, an armoire, white lace curtains with a white eyelet down comforter and pillow shams. This room has its own bath and is sheltered by a lovely cypress tree.

Robbie tells with pleasure of the guests who were married at the nearby Headlands Inn and stayed the night at the Whitegate. (Robbie and Wally were their witnesses.) They're also proud of a recent marriage proposal made here. As well they might be. One could do worse than begin a marriage at this pretty and reasonably priced inn. And I cannot think of better witnesses for a wedding ceremony (or better innkeepers for the honeymoon) than this energetic, winsome, and very solicitous couple.

Country Inn

632 North Main Street
Fort Bragg, California 95437; (707) 964-3737

INNKEEPERS:	*Don and Helen Miller.*
ACCOMMODATIONS:	*Eight rooms, all with private bath; seven queen- and one king-size bed.*
RESERVATIONS:	*Two to three weeks recommended.*
MINIMUM STAY:	*None.*
DEPOSIT:	*First night's lodging.*
CREDIT CARDS:	*MC, VISA.*
RATES:	*Inexpensive to moderate.*
RESTRICTIONS:	*No children. No pets.*

W e may never know for whom this charming structure was built, but we do know it belonged to the Union Lumber Company. In 1893 it was sold to a Mr. L. A. Moody for $500 — a princely sum in those days. (A 1905 edition of the *San Francisco Examiner* found glued to the redwood wallboards here advertises overalls at the bargain price of 17¢ each.)

The building has passed through many hands (and lives) since then. In 1975 Don and Helen Miller moved to Fort Bragg on the craggy Mendocino County coast. Don was working as a free-lance writer, photographer, artisan, and sculptor (he calls himself a one-man advertising agency). He found himself doing a volume business writing and designing brochures for local innkeepers. It occurred to the couple that owning their own bed and breakfast inn would be an ideal way to meet people. And so it has been. (It has also given Helen a chance to pursue one of her favorite avocations: baking bread.)

This is not one of those bed and breakfasts where one is forever afraid to touch anything for fear it might break. Not that the Millers sacrifice the personal touch. Country Inn is appointed throughout with Don's photographs, sculpture, and watercolors. (The skylight in the parlor not only creates excellent light with which to view them, but accentuates the feeling of comfort and relaxation.) I liked the redwood banisters on the stairway and the carefully chosen wallpaper; the exterior is entirely done in redwood paneling.

Each of the bedrooms has plush carpeting, and wallpaper is coordinated with sheets and pillowcases. All of the bathrooms are modern (the attic bedroom has a claw-foot tub, however); one is accessible by wheelchair with special facilities for the handicapped.

Helen makes four delicious varieties of fruit-nut breads (blackberry, banana, lemon, and orange) in addition to honey-corn and honey-wheat muffins. Breakfast also includes melon wedges and slices of other fruits in season, and coffee and orange juice. Don pours complimentary wine in the evening.

Nearby attractions are surprisingly varied in Fort Bragg (a "one-taxi" town). The Footlighter Theater produces locally written musical comedy (usually old-fashioned melodramas in which the audience is encouraged to cheer the fair-haired hero; the villain makes his entrance to boos and hisses). It runs May through August. Fort Bragg is also noted for its many shops and art galleries, gardens, museums — and its award-winning gourmet ice cream.

Don and Helen speak fondly of the couple who were the first to share their accommodations. "We were mortified to find out later that we forgot to put a plug in the bathtub," Don told me. But the Millers needn't have worried — two weeks later their guests sent them a bottle of wine.

I'm not surprised. Making the great escape into total relaxation is not easy to achieve, but the congenial Millers have a formula that works.

Pudding Creek Inn

700 North Main Street
Fort Bragg, California 95437; (707) 964-9529

INNKEEPERS:	*Marilyn and Gene Gundersen.*
ACCOMMODATIONS:	*Ten rooms, all with private bath; twin, double, queen-, and king-size beds.*
RESERVATIONS:	*Two to three weeks recommended.*
MINIMUM STAY:	*Two nights over holidays.*
DEPOSIT:	*First night's lodging. Holidays: In full.*
CREDIT CARDS:	*MC, VISA.*
RATES:	*Inexpensive to moderate.*
RESTRICTIONS:	*No children under twelve. No pets.*

T his very pretty Victorian was built in 1884 by a Russian count who fled the Old World under a cloud. He did not arrive in the New penniless, however; some people were even so uncharitable as to suggest that he had departed with money that was not, legally speaking, his own. Ill-gotten or not, he put his spoils to good use, building seven fine homes in the Fort Bragg area.

In deference to the democratic traditions of his new homeland (and fear of the Russian authorities, probably) our hero changed his name to the less aristocratic — and considerably more anonymous — appellation of Mr. Brown. His wedding was the occasion of considerable local interest: his bride wore the first wedding dress advertised in the Montgomery Ward catalog.

Records reveal that an equally anonymous Mr. Woods and Mrs. White later owned and lived in the count's aging home. In the 1970s it was rescued by Marilyn and Gene Gundersen and restored; in August 1980 it opened as a bed and breakfast inn, its hallways presided over by pictures of the count and his wife.

Actually there are two dwellings; both are two-story buildings connected by an enclosed garden court.

(Breakfast is served here in the summer, and in the antique store—kitchen during winter.) Breakfast consists of juice, fresh fruit, homemade coffee cakes, and coffee or tea. If it is warm weather and you eat outside, you can enjoy the many varieties of fuchsias, begonias, and ferns in the garden court. (Complimentary wine is also served here from 5:00 to 6:00 P.M.)

As we go to press there are a total of ten guest rooms, two of which offer cozy working fireplaces. The Spinning Room is done in yellow and blue, with an old-fashioned spool-design bed. My favorite is the Interlude Room. Shades of Cole Porter's *Blue Room:* everything is blue here (including baby blue), with priscilla curtains. The king-size bed is pecan wood, and there is a spacious bathroom. Altogether a light, sunny and very romantic room that I highly recommend.

A small country store is located in the downstairs of one of the dwellings for your browsing enjoyment. It has collectibles, antiques, and gifts. There are many shops and restaurants nearby. Tennis courts, a logging museum, and the Skunk Train depot are only a few blocks away. There is a Visitors' Center in town to familiarize those who are passing through with the many sights and activities in the community.

This inn is a favorite of at least one well-known character actress. It could become your favorite too. I'm sure the roguish old count who sought refuge in the far reaches of the New World would relish the quiet good taste here — and who could help but applaud the very democratic prices associated with this modern incarnation of his nineteenth-century hideaway?

The Grey Whale Inn

615 North Main Street
Fort Bragg, California 95437; (707) 964-0640

INNKEEPERS:	*John and Colette Bailey.*
ACCOMMODATIONS:	*Thirteen rooms, eleven with private bath; twin, double, queen-, and king-size beds.*
RESERVATIONS:	*Three to four weeks for weekends.*
MINIMUM STAY:	*Two nights over holidays, and on weekends in July and August.*
DEPOSIT:	*First night's lodging; in full for holidays and July/August weekends.*
CREDIT CARDS:	*AE, MC, VISA.*
RATES:	*Inexpensive to moderate.*
RESTRICTIONS:	*No pets (local kennel accommodations).*

Fort Bragg's first (and perhaps its most distinctive) bed and breakfast inn, the Grey Whale, features spacious, comfortable rooms — most with private bath — at very affordable prices. This is an extremely interesting establishment for several different reasons, not the least of which is the discriminating staff. I found a genuine desire to please here, and considerable knowledge about the Fort Bragg area of Mendocino County.

The building itself has long been a landmark, having served from 1915, when it was built, until 1971 as the Redwood Coast Hospital, the north coast's major health-care facility. The weathered redwood siding, completely covering the white clapboard, is trimmed with fresh colors. As more than one observer has noted, it looks as though it had always been an inn — a testament to the skill of those who designed the conversion.

John Bailey worked for Alpha Beta markets, Colette at a Veterans Hospital; both wished to go into business for themselves. They spent a year looking in northern California before they found the right place. (It was advertised in the *Wall Street Journal*.) John enjoys dealing with people in a cooperative, rather than a competitive, way. "One gets positive feedback," Colette says. "The corporate world is a long way from Fort Bragg."

There is a wide variety of rooms here, in terms of size, decor, and views. Hallways are spacious, stairs are easy (guest rooms are on three levels); one bedroom and bath contains accommodations for the handicapped, including ramp access. The Baileys' private collection of art works is displayed throughout the building, with a strong emphasis on work by local artists. (The magnificent whale on the front grounds was carved by Byrd Baker, a leader in the Save the Whales movement.)

Guests are encouraged to let the staff know in advance of special dietary requirements. Breakfast is served from 7:30 to 11:00 A.M. each morning in the Breakfast Room. It includes homemade fruit and nut breads or coffee cake, fresh fruit, hard-cooked eggs, yogurt, or egg custard, and juice and hot beverages. Guests are welcome to take breakfast back to their room.

Guests interested in local activities are supplied with a big book of things to do in the area, easily the most extensive and helpful guide that I saw during my tour. There are a surprising number of attractions: Noyo Harbor with its fishing fleet, state parks and beaches, redwood forests galore, art galleries, concerts, and even good local opera at certain times of the year. (Annual town festivals include the Whale Festival in March, a salmon barbecue in July, and Paul Bunyan Days in the fall.)

One of the most successful bed and breakfast inns I visited, this, and it is easy to see why. It does something that many inns aim for but do not always achieve: it affords the *joie de vivre* of many people gathered under one roof in pleasant surroundings — yet still succeeds, through its conscientious attention to the needs and preferences of the individual, in making each guest feel special.

The Blue Rose Inn

520 North Main Street
Fort Bragg, California 95437; (707) 964-3477

INNKEEPER:	*Anne Samas.*
ACCOMMODATIONS:	*Five rooms, four with private bath; double and queen-size beds.*
RESERVATIONS:	*One month recommended.*
MINIMUM STAY:	*None.*
DEPOSIT:	*First night's lodging.*
CREDIT CARDS:	*AE*
RATES:	*Moderate.*
RESTRICTIONS:	*No children. No pets.*

Anne Samas was raised in southwestern Pennsylvania, and she remembers clearly the popularity of the "guest house." (Motels were once referred to in this part of the country as "motorhotels.") The guest house — or tourist home, as it was sometimes called — was usually a private residence with one or more rooms available to the traveler in search of more personal (and probably less expensive) lodging. Add the breakfast — which many guest houses in Pennsylvania traditionally served — and you have the classic bed and breakfast experience as one generally finds it in Europe and the British Isles.

Anne came to Mendocino in 1962, planning to open a tourist home herself. She priced several houses, but none seemed right. It was not until 1976 that she bought the present structure. It is a ninety-eight-year-old Cape Cod Victorian, and she and her son David have done wonders with it. Her plant-filled establishment is enhanced by redwood ceilings, Tiffany and crystal chandeliers, and attractive wallpaper patterns imported from Korea, Japan, and France.

This is definitely a bed and breakfast inn rather than a private home offering bed and breakfast accommodations, but it exhibits much of the informality of a guest house. Anne's living quarters are in the rear, in an old shed she and David have transformed into a very nice little cottage. She feels this gives guests more elbow room. "Since I'm not technically on the premises, they can do whatever they want," she says. "They have the run of the kitchen and can use the refrigerator, for example." She adds: "When a guest first arrives, I spend some time with him. After that, I'm available — but I don't get in the way."

The rooms — like Anne's garden, which she modestly calls "the best garden in Fort Bragg" — are brightly hued in colors calculated to refresh as well as relax. I liked the French Provincial, which follows a color scheme of gold and lavender. The Blue Room is blue and off-white, with an antique bed of walnut, a marble-topped dresser and washstand, and a claw-foot tub in the bath. (Guests relax in the Green Room, the kitchen, and the parlor — the last-named contains rattan chairs from Taiwan and a fine hand-carved screen.)

Anne is of the opinion that when leaving the toil and turmoil of city life and the working world, one should not continue to punch the time clock. So there is no set time for breakfast: it begins at 8:00 and continues until everybody has finished. Anne sets out quiche, cinnamon-raisin bread, fruit in season, orange juice, milk, and tea and coffee. Guests are supplied with bacon and eggs, which they can make for themselves any time they feel ready for breakfast.

This distinctive laissez-faire policy is also in effect concerning one's departure. The Blue Rose has no check-out time. "Many times guests will still be sitting around the kitchen table talking with other guests over breakfast until noon or even later," Anne says. She makes it clear that this informality is one of the things that make her accommodations friendlier and more relaxed than most — and I heartily agree.

Glass Beach Inn

726 North Main Street
Fort Bragg, California 95437; (707) 964-6774

INNKEEPERS:	*Robert and Beverly Sallinen.*
ACCOMMODATIONS:	*Nine rooms, all with private bath; double and queen-size beds.*
RESERVATIONS:	*Two weeks recommended.*
MINIMUM STAY:	*Two nights on weekends.*
DEPOSIT:	*First night's lodging.*
CREDIT CARDS:	*MC, VISA.*
RATES:	*Moderate.*
RESTRICTIONS:	*Children discouraged. No pets.*

Glass Beach Inn's proprietor, Robert Sallinen, tells of the guest who demanded his money back on arrival. "I told him I was sorry. At breakfast the next day he said he would like to stay a second day." As I see it his change of heart must have been due to one (or perhaps both) of two reasons: a very hearty full breakfast (sausage, bacon or ham, eggs, pancakes, fruits and fruit juices served buffet style, breads or muffins, and coffee or tea); and a totally private (and very relaxing) hot tub available to guests on a "sign up" system.

Guest rooms include the Oriental Jade room, with antique satin and Oriental figurine lamps (wife Beverly is responsible for the interior decoration). The bed is an old-fashioned four-poster; there is a large fireplace to add warmth to your evening. The Victorian Rose features rich, red velvet on the Edwardian double bed, and handsome marble-topped tables.

I opt for Country Comfort, quiet, quaint, and intimate. (Old trunks and rockers, an armoire, a cozy Franklin fireplace, dark blue wallpaper and white lace.) Second choice is Malaysian Experience: cheerful, spacious, and sunny. Wicker furniture and fan-backed chairs add to the Asian atmosphere here. Grandma's Attic is now the largest room in the house. The Schooner Mendocino is the most whimsical: beaded glass windows flanked by dormers, and a bed hanging from ropes attached to the ceiling.

Glass Beach Inn is close to the beach, as well as to the famous Skunk Train. This is an old-fashioned railroad train that takes its passengers deep into the redwood country east of town. There is a half-day trip, as well as a full day's excursion for the more energetic. Beverly and Robert (or Shalome Zahn, the resident manager) will be happy to help you make reservations.

Cobweb Palace Inn

38921 North Highway One; P.O. Box 132
Westport, California 95488; (707) 964-5588

INNKEEPERS:	*Dave Cantley and Peter Husk.*
ACCOMMODATIONS:	*Six rooms, four with private bath; double and queen-size beds.*
RESERVATIONS:	*Three to four weeks recommended.*
MINIMUM STAY:	*Two nights over holidays.*
DEPOSIT:	*First night's lodging plus half of additional nights.*
CREDIT CARDS:	*MC, VISA.*
RATES:	*Inexpensive to moderate.*
RESTRICTIONS:	*No children. No pets.*

Westport is a community of some 150 souls on the Mendocino coast. Ask anyone what to do in Westport, and the answer you'll get is "nothing." Some say that Westport now offers what the town of Mendocino used to: peace and quiet in an environment of near-total isolation. (That is, free of tourists.) And to be sure, Westport does in many ways resemble a much smaller Mendocino, or perhaps the Mendocino of an earlier time.

In keeping with the theme of peaceful isolation, the two innkeepers of the Cobweb Palace follow an enlightened laissez-faire policy toward guests. "We try to leave our guests alone," says Peter, "but without ignoring them." The proprietors complement each other well: if Peter is the more energetic of the pair, Dave is the calm in the eye of the storm. He's originally from Nova Scotia, so this area feels very much like home to him.

It was Dave who found the building. On March 1, 1979 he was an accountant living in Laguna Beach. (Peter was a high school teacher.) He was just about to throw away a newspaper when he felt a "prickly feeling" in his thumb. He looked under it and saw an ad for the sale of a one-hundred-year-old "Victorian Western hotel." The two friends flew up to take a look; a short time later they were in the bed and breakfast inn business.

A true Western Victorian, the building has a false front with boardwalks. It was a hotel originally owned by a local lumber company in the nineteenth century; afterwards it was successively a private residence and a bordello — and finally a hangout of the flower children of the 1960s. It has now been restored to its original glory, in what its new owners call "country comfortable." (The Cobweb Palace's exterior is now painted pewter and dusty coral, accented with white trim.)

A surprisingly homelike atmosphere is encountered within. The Gold Room has a queen-size bed, two comfortable overstuffed rocking chairs, and contemporary furnishings. The Green Room has a sofa and chair in a small sitting area. (Both rooms have a private bath and balcony, overlooking the ocean.) Light gray with pale-pink trim enhances the charm and brightness of other interiors.

Breakfast is fruit compote, muffins (apple, bran, or blueberry), preserves, orange juice, and coffee, tea, or hot chocolate. Breakfast is taken in the bar area from 8:00 to 9:00 weekdays and Saturdays, between 9:00 and 10:00 Sundays.

Cobweb Palace has no TV. Its proud and exacting owners explain its absence in the following way:

> Two things we have for viewing
> That quite surpass TV
> In color, sound and drama:
> Log fires, and the sea.

Howard Creek Ranch

North Highway One, P.O. Box 121
Westport, California 95488; (707) 964-6725

INNKEEPERS:	*Sunny and Sally Lasselle Grigg.*
ACCOMMODATIONS:	*Seven rooms with shared baths; queen-size beds.*
RESERVATIONS:	*One week recommended.*
MINIMUM STAY:	*None.*
DEPOSIT:	*First night's lodging.*
CREDIT CARDS:	*Not accepted.*
RATES:	*Inexpensive to moderate.*
RESTRICTIONS:	*Children discouraged. No pets.*

Howard Creek Ranch might well be described as a bed and breakfast resort. (It has a wood-fired hot tub, a sauna, and a pool set into the side of a mountain, forming a cabana with decks and a massage room.) Yet it also has many characteristics of an inn as well. The ranchhouse is 110 years old, and it has been restored with taste and imagination. The view is as picturesque as any you'll see — located amidst what was once a two-thousand-acre sheep ranch, the land is a vast panorama of mountains descending to grassy slopes that tumble abruptly into the sea.

It was in 1872 that Alfred Howard, newly arrived from Maine, built this ranchhouse. He and his family constructed two houses with the steeply pitched rooflines of the New England coast, and connected them in the middle as is typical in Maine. Thus was created a large, long structure with many bedrooms and lots of space. (One of the upstairs window panes has survived all these years intact, with the name of Lucy Howard — one of the original family members — scratched in the wave of the glass.) The residence was also used as a way station on a stagecoach line during its early years.

The house is built entirely from old-growth redwood and is set in a wide, secluded valley divided by Howard Creek; it faces the beach. (One can walk for miles here during low tide.) The house is filled with antiques, and the original fireplace still warms the parlor. There is something very secure and restful about Howard Creek's thick redwood walls.

The rooms are generally spacious. They range in size, shape, and atmosphere from a loft room in the redwood-paneled attic with a bed under a skylight, to a large and airy suite with an old iron bed and desk in one room and a double bed in another; the suite also has its own kitchen. As a very special extra, Howard Creek has a music room with a piano, an organ, guitars, amplifiers, and microphones, all for guest use.

Sunny Lasselle Grigg was a lighting technician in the film industry before he bought the Howard Creek Ranch in 1972; wife Sally had been traveling in South America, doing research for her degree in community development from Columbia. At first they opened their doors only to friends and people who had heard of them through word of mouth; slowly their home evolved into a bed and breakfast operation.

Breakfast is a full ranch-style meal that includes bacon and eggs. Complimentary wine, beer, cheese, and crackers are served during the day and into the evening.

This area is just south of the Lost Coast, the last undeveloped wilderness area in California. Birds abound in these lovely environs; they include blue herons, hummingbirds, robins, kingfishers, and swallows who migrate to the ranch by the hundreds to build their nests in the barn (the largest on the Mendocino coast). Whales pass by here during winter and summer. In addition to wildlife, horses and cattle graze the fields. (Horses are available to guests who enjoy riding.) Westport Union Landing State Park is nearby, as is Abalone Park, a favorite spot for abalone gathering and rock climbing.

Howard Creek Ranch is an oasis in the wilderness — and it offers reduced rates for long stays as well as midweek and off-season accommodations.

THE GINGERBREAD MANSION

HUMBOLDT COUNTY

101

McKinleyville

The Plough and The Stars

299

Arcata

Old Town Bed & Breakfast Inn
Carter House Inn

Eureka

The Gingerbread Mansion

Ferndale

Alton

36

101

The Gingerbread Mansion

400 Berding Street
Ferndale, California 95536; (707) 786-4000

INNKEEPERS:	*Wendy Hatfield and Ken Torbert.*
ACCOMMODATIONS:	*Four rooms share two baths; twin, double, and queen-size beds.*
RESERVATIONS:	*Three weeks recommended.*
MINIMUM STAY:	*None.*
DEPOSIT:	*Full amount.*
CREDIT CARDS:	*MC, VISA.*
RATES:	*Moderate to expensive.*
RESTRICTIONS:	*No children under ten. No pets.*

Watch that thirteenth step! It's taller than the rest, and purposely designed so to keep evil spirits from ascending the stairway to the upstairs bedrooms. This in strict accordance with Victorian tradition, or rather superstition, carried on to this day at the Gingerbread Mansion in Ferndale.

Billed as northern California's second-most-photographed home, this exquisitely turreted, carved, and gabled mansion with its colorfully landscaped English gardens was originally built as a residence for village physician Dr. Hogan Ring in 1899. It is a visual masterpiece — one of Ferndale's "butterfat palaces" (named for the dairy wealth that built the community), combining Queen Anne and Eastlake architectural styles with an abundance of ornamental trim.

Husband and wife team Ken Torbert and Wendy Hatfield purchased the home-turned-hospital-turned-apartment-house in the spring of 1982 and opened its doors as a bed and breakfast inn just a year later. To date the Gingerbread Mansion has been recognized by an impressive list of publications, including *National Geographic*, *Sunset* magazine, and the *New York Times*.

The inn's four bedrooms, two parlors, and formal dining room are elegantly appointed with antiques of the period. Guest rooms follow various themes and color schemes (the Fountain Room, Rose Room, Garden Room, and Heron Room), but, surprisingly, the most spectacular room in the house is the second-floor bath, with its two hundred square feet of mirrored walls and ceiling, elevated claw-foot tub, French bidet, marble-topped dresser, hanging plants, and floral pastel wallpaper with matching stained-glass window.

The inn's many "little extras" include nightly turn-down service, hand-dipped chocolates by the bedside, bathrobes for the trip down the hall, luggage racks in the rooms, bicycles, a well-stocked supply of information on the area, afternoon tea and cake, and a generous Continental breakfast featuring homemade muffins and breads, assorted cheeses, fresh fruit, orange juice, coffee, and tea.

Ferndale, once known as "cream city," is today touted as "California's best-kept secret." Its well-preserved turn-of-the-century architecture and its Victorian Main Street offering art galleries, an old-fashioned mercantile store, a blacksmith's shop, and even a homemade candy "factory," give it an irresistible fairy-tale charm. Among the fairs, festivals, and parades that perpetuate the enchantment are the Scandinavian Festival, the Humboldt County Fair, a Kinetic Sculpture Race, an Ice Cream Social, and a Pet Parade.

Old Town Bed & Breakfast Inn

1521 Third Street
Eureka, California 95501; (707) 445-3951

INNKEEPERS:	*Floyd and Carol Hall.*
ACCOMMODATIONS:	*Four rooms, three with private bath; twin, double, and queen-size beds.*
RESERVATIONS:	*Two to three weeks recommended.*
MINIMUM STAY:	*None.*
DEPOSIT:	*Full amount.*
CREDIT CARDS:	*MC, VISA.*
RATES:	*Inexpensive to moderate.*
RESTRICTIONS:	*Quiet, well-behaved children only. No pets.*

Humboldt County, located in the northernmost part of California, is a region blessed with a mild climate and natural amenities based on three major resources: conifer forests, rich farmland, and an abundance of water (rivers, bays, and the Pacific Ocean). A fourth, and often unnamed, natural attraction is its people, warm and welcoming.

Eureka is Humboldt's largest city (population twenty-five thousand), and an area that vividly portrays its importance as a major lumber, shipping, and fishing center since the 1850s is Old Town, where restored Victorian buildings on brick-paved walkways house specialty shops and restaurants. The gateway to Old Town is the renowned Carson Mansion at Second and M streets, former home of lumber baron William Carson.

Another one-time residence of the Carson family (from 1872 to 1885), and the last remaining structure of Carson's bay mill, is now a bed and breakfast inn — appropriately Old Town Bed & Breakfast Inn, located at Third and P. This is the house Mrs. Carson loved most, according to local historians, and it's easy to see why. Cute and cozy, its "come on in, relax awhile" feeling is enhanced by present-day owners Floyd and Carol Hall, a couple whose affinity for old houses and new people makes for innkeeping success.

The inn's four guest rooms are decorated with antiques. Two that win my vote of confidence are the Raspberry Parfait Room (plush raspberry carpeting, delicate rose-patterned wallpaper, beige lace curtains, a ruffled comforter on the queen-size bed, and an antique dresser) and the Blue Calico Room (shades of pale blue with frilly white lace curtains, a queen-size bed, and an oak armoire). Whether shared or private, bathroom shelves are amply stocked with the essentials even experienced travelers sometimes leave behind. (A few other pluses: bicycles, inner tubes, complimentary wine and cheese, and late-night dessert.)

Guests convene in the wood-stove-heated kitchen for a hearty breakfast complemented by lively conversation. Belgian waffles are said to be the house specialty, although the entrée might be quiche one morning and pancakes the next. This, along with the home-baked muffins, homemade jams and jellies, fresh fruit in season, and juice, is enough to satisfy until way past noon — which might be about the time you can expect to leave the table. As Floyd says: "You never know who you're going to meet!"

Carter House Inn

Third and L streets
Eureka, California 95501; (707) 445-1390

INNKEEPERS:	*Mark and Christi Carter.*
ACCOMMODATIONS:	*Seven rooms, four with private bath; six double beds and one queen-size bed.*
RESERVATIONS:	*Two to three weeks recommended.*
MINIMUM STAY:	*None.*
DEPOSIT:	*Full amount.*
CREDIT CARDS:	*AE, MC, VISA.*
RATES:	*Moderate to expensive.*
RESTRICTIONS:	*No children. No pets.*

D ear Mom and Dad,

Sophie and I are having a great time up here in Humboldt County. Yesterday we toured the lumber mill at Scotia and drove through the redwoods along the Avenue of the Giants. And you'll never guess what happened. Since we arrived in Eureka earlier than expected, we decided to walk around Old Town and get a look at the Carson Mansion (they say it's the most-photographed house in America) before locating the Carter House Inn. We parked the car and were walking down Third Street when we came alongside of one of the most magnificent Victorian structures I had ever seen. I turned to Sophie and said: "Now *there* is a place I'd like to spend a night!" As we walked around the corner to get a better look I just about died. The sign read: Carter House Inn, Bed & Breakfast.

Mark and Christi Carter are the cutest couple (she's kind of quiet, but just as sweet as can be). Mark told us he built this three-story mansion from plans taken from an 1884 San Francisco Victorian designed by Samuel and Joseph Cather Newsom (same architects as the Carson Mansion) that was destroyed in the 1906 quake. The exterior is constructed of clear heart redwood; the interior is finished in polished redwood and oak.

The first floor serves as a combination contemporary art gallery, antique shop, and common area for the inn. The formal dining room is complete with silver service. There's an ornate wood and marble fireplace, plush velvet upholstered chairs and chaise longues in the parlor, and antiques, pottery, mantel clocks, sculpture, and paintings everywhere. The guest rooms are located on the lower level and the second and third floors. We're staying in the Burgundy Room, which is quite comfortable. Another room I like is the Pink Room, with its late-1800s European oak bedroom set.

We wanted to get over to the Samoa Cookhouse, a family-style restaurant that used to serve up to five hundred lumbermen a day, but the food's so good here there's hardly any room left — wine and hors d'oeuvres at five; tea, cookies, and cordials later in the evening. And Mom, Christi gave me her recipe for that decadent Pecan Phyllo Tart she served at breakfast this morning — along with eggs Benedict, plums with raspberry sauce, bran muffins, a smoked salmon platter, orange juice, and coffee — see what I mean? But you and Dad should really get up here yourselves, I know you'll like it too. See you soon.

Love,
Linda Kay

The Plough and the Stars Country Inn

1800 Twenty-seventh Street
Arcata, California 95521; (707) 822-8236

INNKEEPERS:	*Bill and Melissa Hans.*
ACCOMMODATIONS:	*Five rooms, two with private bath; twin, double and queen-size beds.*
RESERVATIONS:	*Two to three weeks recommended.*
MINIMUM STAY:	*None.*
DEPOSIT:	*First night's lodging.*
CREDIT CARDS:	*Not accepted.*
RATES:	*Inexpensive to moderate.*
RESTRICTIONS:	*No children. No pets.*

I n the midst of all of Humboldt County's Victoriana there is a decidedly refreshing inn with a totally different ambience: The Plough and the Stars Country Inn, named after Irishman Sean O'Casey's play to reflect the proprietors' own ancestry and sentiments.

The inn is an 1860s Midwestern-style farmhouse that sits on two acres. The atmosphere is casual, and the innkeepers are a young enthusiastic pair attempting to "resurrect the proper standard of hospitality."

A series of events guided by the steady hand of fate culminated in this lifetime "dream come true" for Melissa Hans, who saw her first b&b in England at the age of seventeen. She studied hotel and restaurant management at San Francisco's City College while working part-time at the Fairmont and various restaurants around town. Husband Bill, who was employed in timber management for five years, decided to work towards a business degree and is now completing courses at Humboldt State University. Arcata provided the ideal spot for both to accomplish their ambitions.

Part of the attraction of The Plough and the Stars is

the spontaneity and flexibility of its innkeepers. Melissa took me for a swim at the local pool, and the Hanses have been known to take guests out to the beach to watch the sunset when the mood strikes. "We're easy touches for charades and other antics," states Melissa, who has stocked the inn with a full complement of board and parlor games. Family and friends are welcome to visit guests at the inn and share a meal or join in a game of basketball, croquet, or horseshoes. Pastures, lawns, and gardens allow plenty of room for roaming, socializing, and playing, and peaceful country roads invite leisurely jaunts on the inn's bicycles.

In close proximity is Arcata's town center (with one of the few remaining central plazas in California), Humboldt State's campus, and access to Highway 101. Missy's list of "must see's and do's" includes Redwood Park and Community Forest, Arcata's historic walking tour, Moonstone Beach, Fern Canyon, and the Mad River, a favorite fishing spot just a sand dune away. And "don'ts": pay $3 to drive through a tree at Leggett, disregard the "slow to 35 mph" signs, trespass on forestry property, let anyone stick a Trees of Mystery sign on your car's bumper, or leave your swimming suit or raincoat at home.

Early risers ponder the day's activities in the spacious country kitchen over a steaming hot cup of coffee with real cream, the aroma of date-nut bread and blueberry muffins fresh from the oven, and a plate of fresh fruit with slices of cheese. Sleepyheads request breakfast in bed.

Historical, pastoral, homey: three words that merely attempt to describe a feeling too good for words. The Plough and the Stars — not just a place to sleep, rather a suitable place for awakening.

SUTTER CREEK INN

The GOLD COUNTRY

SIERRA

Red Castle Inn

109 Prospect Street
Nevada City, California 95959; (916) 265-5135

INNKEEPERS:	*Chris Dickman and Jerry Ames.*
ACCOMMODATIONS:	*Eight rooms, six with private bath; double beds.*
RESERVATIONS:	*Two weeks recommended.*
MINIMUM STAY:	*Two nights over holidays.*
DEPOSIT:	*Half of full amount.*
CREDIT CARDS:	*Not accepted.*
RATES:	*Moderate to expensive.*
RESTRICTIONS:	*Children discouraged. No pets.*

Imposing is the word for this baronial structure high on Prospect Hill, overlooking the historic Gold Rush town of Nevada City. Four stories high, it is also one of the few classic examples of Gothic Revival — as opposed to the more popular Carpenter Gothic — to be found in the western states. (Gothic Revival was an architectural fashion in the United States from 1835 to 1880; the Red Castle was built in 1859–1860.) Extensive gardens and a pond enhance the castlelike effect; a pathway on the grounds winds to the town below. Double brick walls make the interior considerably cooler on warm days, and add to the feeling of serenity and timelessness.

At 2,800 feet, Nevada City was one of the first towns set up by the forty-niners, who came from all parts of the world looking for the legendary quick strike in the Mother Lode (the Spanish called it the Veta Madre, and the name stuck). Some in fact did make their fortunes in gold; others prospered by furnishing the argonauts — the name by which the gold seekers were most frequently known in the nineteenth century — with basic goods and services. One man who did both was Judge John Williams. Crossing the plains in 1849, he stayed in the booming new city long enough to become a well-known businessman, a mine owner, a civic leader, and finally a judge. After two false starts he succeeded in erecting this monument to his industry. The Red Castle stands today as a reminder of the dreams of glory that motivated all who came to this near-wilderness and stayed to carve out a new state.

In 1963, James Schaar bought and restored the house; his wife managed it later as an inn. In 1978 it was bought by Jerry Ames, formerly a schoolteacher on the Monterey Peninsula, and Chris Dickman, a display coordinator for Macy's. They had seen an ad for the house in *Architectural Digest,* and just two weeks after taking possession opened their doors as a bed and breakfast inn.

The two proprietors have followed a middle course in furnishings. "We want it authentic, but also comfortable," Jerry comments. (The bathrooms retain the old-fashioned washbasins, but stall showers have been added.) The original pine floors and ceiling moldings are exactly as Judge Williams installed them; antiques of the period have been carefully selected for each room. Guest accommodations on the second floor are "parlor suites," each containing a small sitting area as well as a bedroom. Rooms on the first floor open up onto a veranda, and there is a tastefully appointed parlor, complete with old stereoscopic photographs and a viewer. Of special interest are the theatrical masks collected by the owners from all points east, north, south, and west.

Breakfast is date-nut bread or muffins (both homemade), fresh fruit, and fresh-ground coffee. It is served buffet style between 7:30 and 11:30 A.M. Nearby attractions include plenty of gold mines, one of which is open for tours; also musical events, community theater, a bluegrass festival in neighboring Grass Valley, and a classical music event in June. Tahoe National Forest is nearby as well, and it is only thirty-eight miles to Soda Springs.

The *Smithsonian* calls the Red Castle a "perfect restoration," and the Daughters of the Golden West have acknowledged it as an important point of historical interest. It is a place where we come to revel in the gingerbread facade and icicle trim of another era's architectural imagination, but also to relax in the comfortable way its new owners have adapted it to the present.

Mayfield House

236 Grove Street
Tahoe City, California 95730; (916) 583-1001

INNKEEPERS:	*Joanne Neft and Janie Kaye.*
ACCOMMODATIONS:	*Six rooms with shared baths; twin, queen-, and king-size beds.*
RESERVATIONS:	*Two weeks recommended.*
MINIMUM STAY:	*Two nights on weekends in June, July, and August.*
DEPOSIT:	*Half total amount.*
CREDIT CARDS:	*MC, VISA.*
RATES:	*Moderate.*
RESTRICTIONS:	*No children under ten. No pets.*

This reasonably priced and very special bed and breakfast began as the private residence of Norman Mayfield, who built it in 1932. The rooms reflect its history as a residence: Julia's Room commemorates Julia Morgan, a frequent visitor; the Mayfield Room, the builder himself; and the Den, the Study, and Mrs. Hinckle's Room are remembrances of the first principal of a local school who lived here while she pursued her teaching and administrative career.

Joanne Neft once owned and operated a travel agency, and initially envisioned the Mayfield House as an office. In the meantime she traveled as part of her job, and was consistently impressed with the way in which so many hotels seemed to overlook the little "extras" that make one's stay memorable (or even tolerable). The idea of using this warm and stylish home as a bed and breakfast seemed a good one, but at first Mr. Mayfield was not interested in selling. In late 1978 he changed his mind. Joanne took possession May 1, 1979, and opened June 27 — Mr. Mayfield's ninety-first birthday.

The furnishings are mostly original to the house. None are Victorian, but there are some striking Queen Anne and oak pieces, as well as some handsome Empire Revival ones. There is a large stone fireplace with an ample supply of wood. There are no telephones, radios, or televisions, but plenty of rare stonework, pleasant gardens, and beamed ceilings. All rooms have their own library; and down pillows, fresh flowers, and brass and copper accents are the rule. I also liked the original watercolors by Margaret Carpenter. (And the His and Hers velour robes — bravo, Joanne!)

This inn caters to both summer and winter activities — in fact its recreational proximity to skiing is one of the features that make it distinctive. Both cross-country skiing and golf are possible in season just across the street, and guests are within thirty minutes of seventeen downhill ski areas and twelve Nordic ski areas. In the summer guests are just a half block from Lake Tahoe and Commons Beach, as well as shops and restaurants; there is gambling at the state line.

Breakfast at the Mayfield House is exquisite — and different every day. The day I was there that "something different" was Portuguese toast (sweet bread, pan-fried, with fresh fruit sauce), fresh mint from the garden, Danish Havarti cheese, freshly squeezed orange juice, freshly ground coffee, tea, and milk. Mayfield House is also known for its apple strudel, sweet-potato muffins, and Finnish pancakes with strawberry topping and sour cream. Guests can have breakfast in their rooms, on the terrace, in the breakfast room, or even in the homey living room. A newspaper accompanies each breakfast — a small but very accommodating extra.

The Briggs House

2209 Capitol Avenue
Sacramento, California 95816; (916) 441-3214

INNKEEPERS:	*Bob and Sue Garmston, Barbara Stoltz, Kathy Yeates, and Paula Rawles.*
ACCOMMODATIONS:	*Seven rooms, five with private bath; twin, double, and queen-size beds.*
RESERVATIONS:	*Two to three weeks recommended.*
MINIMUM STAY:	*None.*
DEPOSIT:	*First night's lodging.*
CREDIT CARDS:	*AE, MC, VISA.*
RATES:	*Moderate.*
RESTRICTIONS:	*Children in Carriage House only. No pets.*

Doctor William Briggs was born in Ohio and after studying his eye, ear, nose, and throat specialty in Europe, he settled and began his practice in Sacramento. The Capital City was still something of a frontier town in those days. Technically not itself within the Gold Country, it, along with San Francisco, was one of the two centers of civilization toward which the weary miners turned when they were ready to spend their hard-won *nouveaux riches*. So we should not be particularly surprised that Dr. Briggs was the first U.S. medical man to report the "removal of steel from an eye with a magnet," as written by one of his contemporaries. Life was hard in the mining towns, and in the cities it was sometimes brutal and capricious.

But already the Gold Country was slowly turning from mining to more dependable pursuits, among them the lumber business and the embryonic tourism industry. The two are not always compatible callings: Dr. Briggs was one of the original organizers of the Save the Redwoods League, bitterly opposed by the lumber interests. At the same time he was becoming something of a civic leader, a friend of those in high places. In 1901, he bought this cube-type Colonial Revival (Neo-Federalist, if one wishes to be really specific about architectural styles) dwelling, shortly after it was built, and continued to live here until his death in 1931.

What luck, then, that this lively and imaginative quintet got together to restore and manage it as an inn — the first bed and breakfast to open in Sacramento. All the partners are in the same occupation (education), all have different approaches to decorating, yet somehow they managed to make the interiors compatible — despite the fact that each partner decorated a separate room.

The Heritage Suite has a double bed and floor-length tieback drapes in blue, with accessories of the period (lace pillows, perfume bottles, linens, and an old dress hanging on the wall). My favorite was the Sunrise Room, which features a private balcony with white wicker rocker and table which catch the morning sun. It has baby blue walls, armoire, an antique hand-carved double bed, comforter and pillows in beige lace, and a plush carpeted bath.

Guests at the Briggs House are met with linen-lined baskets of fresh fruit and almonds, and wine is served in the parlor in the afternoon (or mineral water, according to one's taste). Breakfast is an elaborate affair served on fine china with silver.

Guests are encouraged to enjoy the large front porch, with its comfortable porch swing. In addition there are the common areas where guests may relax and mingle, if they wish: a well-stocked library, the parlor (once the home's dining room), and a backyard garden — a very pleasant place with its spa and sauna, picnic table, fig and plum trees — framed by redwood lattices. Bicycles are available for pedaling around town. (Sutter's Fort, the Capitol buildings, the Railroad Museum, Old Town, and the Crocker Art Museum are all nearby.)

American River Inn

Main and Orleans streets, P.O. Box 43
Georgetown, California 95634; (916) 333-4499

INNKEEPERS:	*Will and Maria Collin.*
ACCOMMODATIONS:	*Eleven rooms, four with private bath; twin, double, and queen-size beds.*
RESERVATIONS:	*Two to three weeks recommended.*
MINIMUM STAY:	*None.*
DEPOSIT:	*$25.*
CREDIT CARDS:	*AE, MC, VISA.*
RATES:	*Inexpensive to moderate.*
RESTRICTIONS:	*No children. No pets.*

Georgetown is one of those gold country villages that seem to exist in more than one time, the modern starkly accented by visible reminders of the Old West. Cars are parked along the main street — part of which still has the old wooden sidewalk — but it is not at all unusual to see a horse tethered in front of a saloon. It was once a place of quick (if not particularly easy) money, supported by the Woodside Mine, estimated to have brought in $2 million in gold by the spring of 1853. Directly behind the mine was built a spacious rooming house for miners, later a pleasure house with gambling and ladies of the night. Lola Montez, the legendary "spider dancer," once entertained here, according to local history.

The rooming house was also used as a way station by stagecoaches on the Wentworth Springs route to Tahoe. First finished in 1862, it suffered from at least three fires that razed the town during the 1880s, never quite succumbing but requiring partial renovation each time. In recent years it was a private residence and was allowed to decline.

Then it was bought by Al and Marion Podesta, who began the restoration work recently completed by new owners (and bed and breakfast innkeepers) Will and Maria Collin.

Restoration of the historic American River Inn (formerly the American Hotel) turned out to be more difficult (and more lengthy) than anyone could have predicted. (The Podestas were involved with the project for seven years; the Collins managed to finish yet another year's worth of work inside of three months, with a little help from their friends.) Now the dream has come true. The exterior has been painted ivory with Wedgwood-blue trim, and a redwood deck was added for dining *al fresco*. Inside, the red-fir floors have been stripped and refinished, and a floor-to-ceiling rock fireplace was built from native stone (the rooms have ten-foot ceilings). Four cramped rooms downstairs were turned into two; upstairs guest rooms have been furnished with wainscoting, crown moldings, and ornamental mopboards.

Breakfast at the American River Inn is always a treat. Maria makes it a point never to serve any guest the same breakfast twice. The morning I was there I was privileged to receive quiche Lorraine, Canadian bacon, blueberry muffins, orange juice, and cinnamon coffee. (Neal and Carol La Morte, who share innkeeping duties with the Collins, have a specialty all their own: a full country breakfast with eggs "any way you like them," fresh link sausages, and country-fried potatoes.)

Guests may relax in either the dining room or the parlor with its Franklin stove and player piano. Outside is the aviary, a vegetable garden, a swimming pool, and a heated Jacuzzi.

Nearby attractions include the Ponderosa Saloon (next door), twelve lakes "up country," and good fishing and gold panning. But this is essentially a place to get away from activities, not to explore new ones. As for interesting goings-on in the area, I was told the Scotch broom blooms in April and May. Let's just say that if you're feeling lost, the American River Inn is a place where you can begin to find your way back.

The Fleming Jones Homestead

3170 Newtown Road
Placerville, California 95667; (916) 626-5840

INNKEEPER:	*Janice Condit.*
ACCOMMODATIONS:	*Five rooms, three with private bath; double beds.*
RESERVATIONS:	*One month recommended for weekends.*
MINIMUM STAY:	*None.*
DEPOSIT:	*First night's lodging, weekdays; total amount, weekends and holidays.*
CREDIT CARDS:	*Not accepted.*
RATES:	*Inexpensive to moderate.*
RESTRICTIONS:	*No children under twelve. No pets.*

This delightful two-story, nineteenth-century farmhouse was the first bed and breakfast inn on the western side of the Sierra foothills of El Dorado County. It's a good bet for those who seek total relaxation. No televisions, radios, not even a telephone — but there are eleven acres to relax and ramble in. Since the Fleming Jones Homestead is also a working farm, eggs and homemade preserves are for sale, there are pet chickens and burros, and pasture is available to those who enjoy giving their horses a vacation, too.

The Joneses were a pioneer family who settled in the area in the 1850s. Fleming Jones reputedly financed this home for his wife Florence with gambling money. She had wanted a new house for some time, when (according to family legend) Fleming came home late one night from a saloon where he was part owner. His cards had been lucky that night, and his pockets were full of money — which he promptly set down in front of his astonished wife. "There," he said. "Go build your house!"

Florence obeyed with alacrity. She had her new home built entirely of "clear" lumber — that is, planks without knots in them; it was completed in 1883.

When Janice Condit began to renovate the old farmhouse, she asked Fleming Jones's granddaughter if she might use his name. The granddaughter was more than happy to give the venture her blessing. It's easy to see why — this is a respectful yet very comfortable venture into the homestead's past, one that respects its tradition as a working farm. (Janice lives in an old milk house that has been imaginatively converted into living quarters, adjacent to the main dwelling.)

All rooms are decorated with country antiques. Lover's Fancy is done in tones of peach and white, with an iron and brass bed. The Rose Room looks out onto a rose garden. (The historic rose garden, adjacent to the farmhouse, includes more than one hundred rosebushes — mostly of the "old rose" varieties such as damasks, gallicas, and rugosas.) The bed here has a hand-carved oak headboard. The Flower Basket Room opens onto the second-floor balcony, and the Bunk House is just that — rustic on the outside, as warm and charming inside as a cottage — decorated with all sorts of old lamps, farm implements, and homestead treasures.

The parlor beckons with two corner rockers, and a variety of books, unusual periodicals, and sherry on the library table await your pleasure. Porches with swings and comfortable chairs overlook the homestead vegetable garden and adjoining meadows. Hikers can inspect the remains of mining equipment, mute testimony to the men who searched for gold here long ago.

Janice calls her breakfast "expanded Continental": homemade hot breads, rolls or muffins, farmhouse preserves, fruit breads, fresh fruit — including pears and apples from the orchard — sweet butter, and tea or fresh-ground French roast coffee. It is served at a massive table in the dining room that reminded me of the big tables at which my grandmother once fed my grandfather's threshing crews. If you've never had a grandmother with a farm in the country, a leisurely visit here will show you what you've missed — and once you've experienced that, you'll surely want more of the same.

Mine House Inn

South Highway 49, P.O. Box 245
Amador City, California 95601; (209) 267-5900

INNKEEPERS:	*Ann Marie and Peter Daubenspeck III.*
ACCOMMODATIONS:	*Eight rooms, all with private bath; double beds.*
RESERVATIONS:	*Two weeks recommended.*
MINIMUM STAY:	*None.*
DEPOSIT:	*First night's lodging.*
CREDIT CARDS:	*Not accepted.*
RATES:	*Inexpensive.*
RESTRICTIONS:	*No pets.*

A mador means "love of gold" — and more than half the gold mined and panned during the boom years of the Gold Rush came from Amador County. It was here in Amador City that one of the first large gold quartz mining claims was staked out, in 1850. In 1851 the Keystone Consolidated Mine was formed, its total production eventually to exceed $24 million. The Mine House Inn is located in the old mine headquarters, a solid brick structure built in 1867, during the days when any mine headquarters was a likely target for bandits and highway robbers.

Peter Daunbenspeck had been in the hotel business in San Francisco for eleven years when he decided to manage the old Consolidated headquarters as an inn; the building itself had been in his family for almost three decades. It is the only inn in America housed in such a structure. It is also one of the few bed and breakfast inns in the area that accepts children, a welcome accommodation for the traveling family. And it is the only one hereabouts that has a swimming pool for the guests' enjoyment.

Peter has carefully furnished his inn with antiques that all come from the Mother Lode, within a hundred-mile radius of Mine House. The decor and ambience of the rooms make this place noteworthy.

The theme of each room is keyed to its original function. In the Mill Grinding Room, for example, one finds the shaft supports still in the ceiling (these held the shafting used to drive the machinery for pulverizing the sample ore prior to assaying).

The Vault Room was actually once the huge safe in which all bullion was stored prior to shipping via Wells Fargo Stage to San Francisco. The Retort Room was where millions of dollars' worth of gold was smelted into gold bullion and carried by dumbwaiter to the vault. (The arch supporting this vault still remains.) The Stores Room with its warm red brick walls was where rock picks, tallow candles, and flasks of quicksilver were stored. The Directors' Room — with its high ceiling and private entrance to the front balcony — was where the affairs of the company were talked over, and profits were divided among mine owners and operators.

Orange juice, coffee, tea, and hot chocolate are available in the morning. The real attractions are the historical interest of the building, the reasonable rates, and the imaginative rendering of the rooms. It's also a good place for walking — Amador City has more than its share of historic buildings — and is centrally located for those who wish to explore some of the old mine sites. (In addition to Keystone Consolidated, the Plymouth Consolidated, the Central Eureka, the Kennedy, and the Argonaut mines are all within five miles of the Mine House Inn.)

The Foxes

77 Main Street
Sutter Creek, California 95685; (209) 267-5882

INNKEEPERS:	*Pete and Min Fox.*
ACCOMMODATIONS:	*Three suites; queen-size beds.*
RESERVATIONS:	*Four weeks recommended for weekends.*
MINIMUM STAY:	*Two nights on weekends and holidays.*
DEPOSIT:	*First night's lodging.*
CREDIT CARDS:	*AE, MC, VISA.*
RATES:	*Moderate to expensive.*
RESTRICTIONS:	*No children. No pets.*

T his is one of those places that remind one of the European bed and breakfast spots. But it's more than just a couple of spare rooms; these are luxury suites, each intended to accommodate two people. (Because one is private and intimate in atmosphere, it is called the Honeymoon Suite. The proprietors — Pete and Min Fox — don't insist that their guests be honeymooners, but I can't think of a nicer place to spend one's honeymoon than in this intimately furnished little love nest.)

This charming two-story Victorian was once known locally as the Brinn House. It was built by Morris Brinn and his brother in 1857. Like so many who prospered during the Gold Rush, they sought their fortunes not in mines and gold pans, but in supplying the miners with the basic necessities of life in a gold camp: they owned a dry goods store in Sutter Creek, and a fairly large one at that. Their fine home has a definite New England flavor to it, typical of many of the old homes in this area and reflecting the origins of many of the settlers.

What is remarkable is that this quintessential Gold Rush Victorian was allowed to stand vacant for twenty-five years. In the 1960s it was rescued by a couple who began its restoration; later it was owned by another couple who continued the work and served lunch in a luncheon room in the building. The Foxes have now had it for four years, and the old Brinn residence has never looked better in its 127 years.

Their Honeymoon Suite consists of a sitting room, a bedroom, and a private bath. The bed has an amazing nine-foot-high headboard, and there is a matching marble-topped dresser (also nine feet tall) of walnut and walnut burl, circa 1875. The bedspread is a floral print coordinated with an antique floral-stripe wallpaper and the sheer drapes, which are tied back with a matching floral fabric. There is a Queen Anne love seat in the sitting room and another Queen Anne piece — a fine writing desk — that doubles as a breakfast table.

Breakfast at the Foxes is flexible. "Since there are only three couples to consider," Min says, "we can talk about it once they get here." A typical breakfast might be fresh-squeezed orange juice, a very large fruit platter, eggs with ham, bacon, or sausage, sourdough French toast or blueberry muffins, and your choice of hot beverage.

Both Min and husband Pete come from Orange County. They got into the bed and breakfast business almost by accident. Pete had been in real estate for many years and envisioned the Brinn place as a possible office. The couple who were selling the house liked the Foxes' plan to open an antique shop there, but also spoke glowingly of the possibility of furnishing and renting a suite.

It was a natural. Min Fox well remembers her first customer. Jane Way of the neighboring Sutter Creek Inn called to say that a honeymoon couple had reserved the room, but in the bustle and rush of wedding arrangements had forgotten to mail their deposit. Could the Foxes put them up for a night? They could, and did. The next morning the bride and bridegroom watched the annual Italian Picnic Day parade from the Foxes' porch. "They got very emotional when they left," Min recalls. "And they came back for their first wedding anniversary. Since then we've become close friends."

There is nothing like a bed and breakfast inn to launch a new marriage — or to invigorate one that has been around a while. And there is no inn that I would recommend more highly for this than the Foxes'.

Sutter Creek Inn

75 Main Street
Sutter Creek, California 95685; (209) 267-5606

INNKEEPER:	*Jane Way.*
ACCOMMODATIONS:	*Seventeen rooms, all with private bath; twin, double, and queen-size beds.*
RESERVATIONS:	*Flexible, but phone as early as possible.*
MINIMUM STAY:	*Two nights on weekends.*
DEPOSIT:	*$50 a day per room.*
CREDIT CARDS:	*Not accepted.*
RATES:	*Moderate.*
RESTRICTIONS:	*No children under fifteen. No pets.*

Huge lawns surround this deservedly well-known inn, and in summer garden furniture and hammocks are a delight under the redwood and laurel trees. An old and stately grape arbor is a haven for those who like to play cards during the day. Many fine restaurants are within walking distance of the inn and proprietor Jane Way keeps a book with guests' comments on local eating spots. Sutter Creek is itself a kind of living museum of architecture from 1860 to 1920. (If you wish to explore the town on foot, it is suggested that you pick up a copy of *Stroller's Guide to Sutter Creek* at the Tyler card shop on Main Street.)

Sutter Creek Inn was originally built as a Greek Revival by one of the town's leading businessmen, a man named Keyes, using redwood but following the style then current in New England. (It was a wedding gift to his homesick bride, a woman from New Hampshire.) It was owned later by State Senator Edward Voorheis, who married the Keyses' daughter in 1880. It was still in the possession of the same family when it was spotted by Jane Way, on a pleasure excursion through the gold country with her children. She fell in love with it instantly. After two months of calling daily, she convinced the family she would be a worthy new owner of the historic building. "It's been well cared for," Jane says proudly, "and it's sturdy as a rock."

There is a large living room, with sherry on the sideboard. The color here is robin egg blue, and there are some Oriental pieces that go quite well with the country antiques. The large sofas are upholstered in floral prints, and I particularly liked the hutch with antique china and the grandfather clock. There is a very large library with current magazines and literally thousands of books, as well as a piano for the musical. Jane is a talented handwriting expert and will read your palm as well as your handwriting for character traits.

Jane is interested in psychic experiences — and it was perhaps because of that openness that she was once visited by a ghost. He was a distinguished-looking gentleman who said simply, "I will protect your inn!" and vanished. (Jane thinks he might have been Senator Voorheis.) Certainly he would be proud of her country kitchen, with its partially paneled brick walls, copper colanders, impressive collection of guns, and Oriental rug.

Many guest rooms are in what used to be outbuildings. Most have a distinctly country feeling, but are done with Jane's exquisite and quite sophisticated taste. Some rooms have patios; most have small libraries. Many have fireplaces, and one that I particularly liked contained a table made from a bass drum. Ceiling beams, canopy beds, and samplers are the rule in other rooms. Four of the rooms have beds suspended from the ceiling by chains and cables.

Jane likes variation in her breakfast menu, but a typical day's fare might consist of crispy fried potatoes with bacon and onions, sliced fresh fruit, buttermilk pancakes with raw apples and walnuts, and soft scrambled eggs with parsley.

At one time she stayed up each night to give guests a nightcap of brandy, but claims they kept her up too late. Now guests receive brandy in their morning coffee, if they so wish. If you *don't* wish, be sure to tell her, because Jane is as generous with her spirits as she is with her highly personable brand of vivacious hospitality.

Nine Eureka Street

9 Eureka Street, P.O. Box 386
Sutter Creek, California 95685; (209) 267-0342

INNKEEPER:	*Marie Sanders.*
ACCOMMODATIONS:	*Five rooms, four with private bath; queen-size beds.*
RESERVATIONS:	*Flexible.*
MINIMUM STAY:	*Two nights on holiday weekends.*
DEPOSIT:	*$35.*
CREDIT CARDS:	*Not accepted.*
RATES:	*Moderate.*
RESTRICTIONS:	*No children on weekends; school-age children welcome on weekdays. No pets.*

The Lagomarsino clan were early settlers in the gold country, arriving in 1856. One of many industrious Italian-Americans who helped build up this area, Tobias Lagomarsino and certain other family members operated a stagecoach route on the Sutter Creek, Jackson, and Volcano line. It was not until 1916, however, that the family built this modest but very nice New England—flavored dwelling in the second block of two-block-long Eureka Street, just off Main Street.

The Lagomarsino home is now operated as a very comfortable bed and breakfast by Marie Sanders. The rooms are individually decorated in the mode of the past, but there is also air conditioning — not a minor consideration some summer evenings. The rooms are large, the atmosphere gracious; the tendency here is toward china and crystal, good silver, and linen napkins. Yet the ambience remains homey. I particularly liked the large porch, with its view of the surrounding hills.

Marie had been in the hotel business in San Francisco for three years when she heard that this California-style cottage was for sale. "And it was a *lot* of work," Marie acknowledges. But she has done very well, mixing English antiques with turn-of-the-century local ones. My favorite room is one that used to be a sleeping porch (now called the Gold Room). Windows on all three sides give it a light and airy feeling that is very refreshing.

The dining room sports chandeliers, leaded and stained glass windows, and elm wainscoting. The sitting room (which merges into the dining area) features beamed ceilings, plush carpets, and contemporary furnishings. The sitting room closes at 10:00 P.M., but until then Marie invites you to "browse among the many books and revive the gentle art of conversation."

Breakfast is expanded Continental fare: fresh orange juice, fruit compote, a coddled egg, homemade muffins, coffee, tea, or milk.

Sutter Creek is centrally located in the gold country. There is excellent fishing at the well-stocked low-elevation lakes: Camanche, Pardee, and Amador. Fairs, rodeos, and local festivals are the rule in summer. Kirkwood Meadows, one of California's best ski areas, is not far away. Or you may simply wish to drive around the back roads leading away from Highway 49. From Main Street, drive up Sutter Hill Road past the abandoned Botto Saloon and the Central Eureka Mine, or along Amador Road, past the Union-Lincoln mine site. These and other byways leading from Sutter Creek are lined with ancient stone walls and occasional crumbling stone buildings from the Mother Lode's colorful past.

Court Street Inn

215 Court Street
Jackson, California 95642; (209) 223-0416

INNKEEPER:	*Mildred Burns.*
ACCOMMODATIONS:	*Seven rooms, four with private bath; twin, double, and queen-size beds.*
RESERVATIONS:	*Two weeks recommended.*
MINIMUM STAY:	*None.*
DEPOSIT:	*First night's lodging.*
CREDIT CARDS:	*Not accepted.*
RATES:	*Moderate to expensive.*
RESTRICTIONS:	*No children. No pets.*

T he main part of this house was built in 1870 for the Isaac Peiser family, on what was then called Corral Hill. (Apparently the area was used for grazing cattle in those early days.) Only three years later Mr. Peiser and his young son died, victims of diphtheria. The remainder of the wealthy merchant's family continued to live here until the house was sold to the Blairs, who owned the Jackson Water Works, and their daughter Grace Depue.

The Miwok Indians in this area were frequently unable to pay their water bills in cash, so they made payments in the form of baskets and other artifacts. Grace Depue kept the collection in a brick house in the back (now called the "Indian House," where two of the inn's guest rooms are located); in her will she donated it to Stanford, and at the time of her death it was appraised at $90,000. In this way a priceless collection of Miwok folk art was preserved for the enjoyment of all Californians.

Mildred Burns had visited the gold country frequently from her home in San Luis Obispo, vacationing at bed and breakfast inns. She was looking for a way to make a living, and to take care of aging parents at the same time. The present dwelling seemed to have everything: it was a home of the Victorian era, with a small house in back for her parents. Restoration began in May

1980; the first guests arrived before work was even finished, in April 1981.

That first week a woman called from Sacramento. She wanted to be married in Jackson — could she have three rooms for the wedding party? "And that was on only two days' notice," Mildred points out. "Before it was over I ended up finding a minister for them, and we had the wedding right here in the parlor. *And* the reception." It was Mildred's blunt introduction to a certain fact of life: the proprietor of a bed and breakfast inn often doubles as a social secretary.

My favorite room at Court Street (which is now on the National Register of Historic Places) is the Peiser Room. It has its own sun porch, a sitting area with wicker pieces, old quilts, and fresh flowers, and some fine Queen Anne furniture; the colors here are pink and white. (There are also ruffled pillow shams and a pitcher and washbowl.)

There are Oriental pieces throughout the house: rugs, ginger jars, and, in the larger parlor, a lovely lacquered Chinese screen. (Mildred explains that these kinds of pieces — particularly Chinese screens — were widely used during Victorian days.)

Despite what Mildred calls the "Early American Gold Rush" ambience of her carefully designed and decorated rooms, all of them are air-conditioned. Complimentary wine (or tea) is served in the guest rooms, sherry in the parlor. A full breakfast is served at Court Street Inn: French toast, granola, strawberries and yogurt, homemade breads (including pumpkin-banana nut), egg dishes, crêpes and quiches, orange juice, and tea or coffee. All are made especially enjoyable by the friendly company of your hostess and proprietor, a unique woman who combines vivacity with character — an admirable compound that seems especially appropriate to this very magical part of California.

Ann Marie's Lodgin and Gallery

410 Stasel Street
Jackson, California 95642; (209) 223-1452

INNKEEPER:	*Ann Marie Joseph.*
ACCOMMODATIONS:	*Three rooms, all with private bath; twin and double beds.*
RESERVATIONS:	*One to two months recommended.*
MINIMUM STAY:	*None.*
DEPOSIT:	*First night's lodging.*
CREDIT CARDS:	*Not accepted.*
RATES:	*Moderate.*
RESTRICTIONS:	*No pets.*

Ann Marie Joseph was raising her children alone, working two jobs for very little money; yet she was a frustrated writer and painter. Her dilemma was the ancient struggle between the needs of the creative artist and the more prosaic needs of society at large. How could she realize her creative ambitions and still make enough money to feed her children (and herself) in this area of somewhat limited employment and business opportunity? She decided that a bed and breakfast was the answer, and got herself a job with another local inn to see how the business end worked.

"I saw a lot of families being turned away because they had children," Ann Marie says; and since she is a mother, she naturally finds herself sympathetic to those with "little folks." So it should be no surprise that she encourages families. It is not unusual for large families to book more than one room, and Ann Marie will arrange for a babysitter for infants and young children for a very reasonable $3 an hour.

Built in 1892, this Victorian was used by Dr. James Wilson both as a personal residence and as an office for his patients, most of whom were miners and their families. Ann Marie has furnished it throughout with country pieces, most of which she found in the 1960s.

"In those days it was called junkin', not antiquein'," she points out. The rest of the antiques are from her Portuguese grandparents. The parlor and sitting room contain her quilts and handsewn stitchery, as well as a wood-burning stove; out back there is a garden swing for the young and the young at heart.

Rooms are named after their original functions in Ann Marie's residence. Mama's Room is my favorite: an antique brass bed, lace curtains, a private bath with a claw-foot tub, and an old-fashioned beveled, mirrored bird's-eye maple dresser all add to the atmosphere of quiet country leisure. There is also an antique trunk that belonged to her kids' grandparents, who brought it with them around the Cape on their long passage to the New World.

One unusual and very pleasing aspect of this inn is the original art on the walls. Many of the paintings are Ann Marie's. ("And people actually buy 'em," she remarks cheerily.) Works of Sutter Creek artist Joan Tarr and local copper handcrafter Gerry Raddatz are also displayed.

Ann Marie's Continental breakfast usually features fruits in season, juice, milk, hot chocolate, and coffee. In the evening guests receive complimentary iced tea or wine; hot toddies are served in the winter. Homemade pastries and baskets of fruit await you in the dining room; there's soda in the fridge and brandy in the parlor.

Ann Marie says, "I have the best of both worlds now, the world of work and the world of creativity." Which is not surprising, as this energetic and youthful woman is blessed with talent in both areas.

Gate House Inn

1330 Jackson Gate Road
Jackson, California 95462; (209) 223-3500

INNKEEPERS:	*Frank and Ursel Walker.*
ACCOMMODATIONS:	*Five rooms, all with private bath; double and queen-size beds.*
RESERVATIONS:	*Two to three weeks recommended.*
MINIMUM STAY:	*Two nights on weekends, April through October.*
DEPOSIT:	*$35.*
CREDIT CARDS:	*Not accepted.*
RATES:	*Moderate.*
RESTRICTIONS:	*No children. No pets.*

T he Gate House seems to loom larger than life on Jackson Gate Road. Inside, its ten-foot ceilings, solid-oak parquet floors, original wall coverings, chandeliers, marble fireplace, and hints of Oriental influence bespeak Gold Country. And Gold Country it certainly is. This turn-of-the-century Victorian is located near the historic Kennedy Mine on the outskirts of Jackson, a mid–Mother Lode city and the seat of Amador County since 1854.

The two-story house, entered through a wrought-iron gate, was built by the Chichizola family, the first general merchants of the area. Structurally speaking it is one of only two Victorians of this quality in Amador County, which allowed Frank and Ursel Walker (second owners of the property after the original family) to open it as a bed and breakfast inn shortly after their purchase in 1981.

For four years previous to their purchase the Walkers had watched the operation of the Sutter Creek Inn while serving its clientele from the Palace, a restaurant they owned across the street. This inn-spiration proved worthy, and their culinary talents are not wasted here. A typical breakfast starts off with a beautifully displayed fresh-fruit salad of watermelon, cantaloupe, pineapple, blackberries, and grapes served on English bone china. This is followed by a scrumptious lemon-cinnamon coffee cake with hot applesauce, coddled eggs, a stemmed glass of fresh orange juice with a slice of banana, coffee, and sweet apple-spice tea. Fresh flowers and a white lace tablecloth grace the formal dining table. Breakfast commences at the stroke of 9:00.

Of special interest are the more than one hundred clocks Frank has collected over the past ten years. Included are grandfather clocks, shelf clocks, and wall clocks, from points as distant as Germany and France and as close to home as Sutter Creek. A Santa Fe railroad clock that once hung in the Albuquerque, New Mexico, telegraph office now passes the time of day in the inn's Parlor Room.

Gate House Inn's most popular guest room (in terms of price and size) is at the top of the stairs — the Brass Room, aptly named for its queen-size brass and onyx bed. My favorite, though, was the Woodhaven Suite, which according to Ursel is the room of choice of the journalists, feature writers, authors, and inn reviewers who come through. This wood-paneled suite that resembles a loft intimates seclusion. Its brass bed with a delicate floral-print comforter in beige and brown, and a large oval braided rug enhance the cozy, tucked-away feeling. It also has a separate sitting room with red-rose wallpaper, a leather sofa-bed to accommodate a third person, and a display case of shelf clocks.

Assorted niceties I particularly liked: starched and ironed bed linens; bubble bath and a rubber ducky; portraits from the Victorian era by southern California artist J. Pajares; a swimming pool, a barbecue, and a greenhouse; and — within walking distance of the inn — four fine restaurants, as well as dancing on Friday and Saturday nights.

The Heirloom

214 Shakeley Lane
Ione, California 95640; (209) 274-4468

INNKEEPERS:	*Patricia Cross and Melisande Hubbs.*
ACCOMMODATIONS:	*Four rooms, one with private bath; twin, double, queen-, and king-size beds.*
RESERVATIONS:	*Two to three weeks recommended.*
MINIMUM STAY:	*None.*
DEPOSIT:	*First night's lodging.*
CREDIT CARDS:	*Not accepted.*
RATES:	*Inexpensive to moderate.*
RESTRICTIONS:	*No pets.*

P art of California's fascination is due to the diversity of its people. This is reflected in its variety of architectural styles — particularly in the Gold Country, where people from many parts of the country converged at once. A good example of this is the Heirloom, a bed and breakfast inn in Ione. Obviously built by a Southerner, this two-story brick Colonial mansion with an antebellum arch replicates perfectly the prevailing fashion in the South before the Civil War.

Built in 1863 by a Virginian (who also built another Southern-style mansion in Ione), the structure was soon purchased by Dr. Luther Brusi, who in 1870 was a veteran of the Confederacy. He must have felt very much at home in this lovely dream house, with its stately columns, verandas, and white-wood balconies. Somewhat later it was sold to James and Catherine Browning (Catherine remained here until 1923); James was associated with the famous Browning rifle company.

The house was purchased by Patricia Cross and Melisande Hubbs in 1980. Both had been looking around Sonoma and Carmel for a dwelling appropriate for a bed and breakfast, when they heard of this place. Ione is somewhat off the tourist track; it was never a boom town, but a supply center for the mining camps. Yet when they saw this undeniably breathtaking structure they knew it was the right one for them.

All windows are deep-set in the Southern style. (The house and garden are completely hidden from public view by shrubs and trees.) The front entrance boasts a fan transom. The living room is completely paneled in wood painted off-white, as was the custom in early days. The high ceiling and paneled windows (draped in gold brocade), stained pine floor with area rugs, Colonial staircase and mantel are an elegant background to the antique furnishings in this very livable mansion.

Pat and Melisande are quite flexible toward guests; one is not encumbered with a surfeit of rules and regulations here. "I like to see the tension melt out of people's faces after they've been in the country a while," says Melisande. One of the pieces they are most proud of is their grand piano, once the possession of Lola Montez, famed "Gold Rush queen" of Grass Valley. This instrument has an offset keyboard and heavy, beautifully carved rosewood legs.

The rooms are named for the seasons. The Winter Room has a fireplace; burgundy and pale-blue tones predominate. The Spring Room, in yellow and green, has lovely handmade quilts, an old-fashioned rocker, and gay white wicker furniture. The Autumn Room has a brass bed, a comforter, and pillow shams with matching duet ruffles. The Summer Room features pink rose wallpaper, cool green and beige tones, a queen-size bed, and a very nice Queen Anne desk.

Sherry, white wine, or tea is served in the early evening, and guests find fresh flowers, fruit, and candy in their rooms. Breakfast is full — and very generous. On a typical morning you will receive fresh-squeezed orange juice, crêpes with fresh fruit topping, popovers and croissants, cheese (Brie), and gourmet coffee from Louisiana. In keeping with the Southern theme, Pat and Melisande usually serve breakfast wearing long aprons and skirts, adding to the sense of calm and antebellum luxury that is so much a part of the Heirloom.

Dunbar House

271 Jones Street, P.O. Box 1375
Murphys, California 95247; (209) 728-2897

INNKEEPERS:	*John and Barbara Carr.*
ACCOMMODATIONS:	*Five rooms share two baths; double and queen-size beds.*
RESERVATIONS:	*Three weeks recommended.*
MINIMUM STAY:	*None.*
DEPOSIT:	*First night's lodging.*
CREDIT CARDS:	*Not accepted.*
RATES:	*Moderate.*
RESTRICTIONS:	*No children under ten. No pets.*

T his lovely Italianate Victorian with its white siding and blue shuttered windows, wraparound veranda, and white picket fence reminds one of a set from an old western and was, in fact, used in filming the TV version of MGM's *Seven Brides for Seven Brothers*. It reflects a man of means of its time: Willis Dunbar, who built the house for his bride Ellen in 1880. Dunbar was a prominent citizen in the community, a superintendent of the water company, and at one time served a turn in the State Assembly. Murphys was a boom town then; a magnet drawing fortune seekers who discovered some of Calaveras County's richest placer gold claims here. Today historical Main Street, just steps from the inn, affords seekers of a different sort a well-preserved glimpse into the past of this "Queen of the Sierra."

For John and Barbara Carr the flight to Murphys represented a change of gears — a transition from the "rat race," as they called it, to a better quality of life. The Carrs were living in Palo Alto, but spending a good many weekends in the Gold Country. They found it harder to return home each time. When this property, which housed an antique shop, came up for sale, they couldn't resist. Now happily settled, John serves the community as a volunteer fireman, and Barbara, who comes from a twenty-year nursing career, is the Sunshine

Lady for the local chapter of the American Association of University Women. Her duties include sending get-well cards to ailing fellow members.

The five guest rooms here have several antiques, but, as Barbara says, obviously not of any particular period. Eclectic hominess, she calls it. Flowers and doilies are much in evidence; beds are turned down while guests are out to dinner. Electric blankets and fluffy comforters keep you warm in winter; there is air conditioning in summer. Pine-needle baskets, handicrafts, and original watercolors scattered throughout the house show off the talents of local artists. Books, games, a stereo set, and a TV are located in the parlor. "Guests are welcome to watch the news," says Barbara, "but advised not to get into the late movie."

Old photographs of the Dunbar family and historical events pertinent to the house grace the walls of the dining room, the scene of an ample buffet-style breakfast. Included are two or three cold cereals with milk, homemade banana-nut bread and pumpkin-spice muffins, fruit compote, an assortment of cheeses, orange juice, coffee, tea, and hot chocolate. Breakfast is served between 8:30 and 9:15, but the coffee is on by 8:00.

A side table full of brochures advertising area attractions sits by the door. Pick up a few on your way out, as I'm sure you'll want to get a good start on the day. I'd recommend a couple of hours at Calaveras Big Trees State Park; stop at the Quyle Kilns on your way up to buy some local pottery. Moaning Cavern and Mercer Caverns offer guided tours; Stevenot Winery is open for wine tasting; downhill and cross-country skiing is just forty-five minutes away; antique and gift shops, as well as fine dining, are just a block away. Annual celebrations include St. Patrick's Day, the Murphys Homecoming in July, an Octoberfest, and performances by the Black Bart Players in April and November.

Llamahall Guest Ranch

18170 Wards Ferry Road
Sonora, California 95370; (209) 532-7264

INNKEEPER:	*Cindy Hall.*
ACCOMMODATIONS:	*Two rooms, each with private bath; twin and queen-size beds.*
RESERVATIONS:	*Two to three weeks recommended.*
MINIMUM STAY:	*None.*
DEPOSIT:	*First night's lodging.*
CREDIT CARDS:	*Not accepted.*
RATES:	*Moderate.*
RESTRICTIONS:	*No pets.*

N ow *here* is a stay with a difference — Llamahall Guest Ranch, home of Cindy Hall, her two children, and their pet llamas, Lady Love and Lickity Spit.

Cindy, a fireball of energy, is an innkeeper, mother, rancher, antique dealer, interior decorator, and intrepid aeronaut (an FAA certified hot air balloon pilot). She and current partner Kristin Moore say they have the only bb&b (bed, breakfast, and balloon ride) around.

Don't expect to be pampered and doted on here. This is not to say that the accommodations aren't pleasant — they are. It's just that this is Cindy's home, and guests become the secondary consideration rather than the primary. Breakfast, for example, was served *after* Cindy had got the kids off to school.

Not to be dismayed, though, as there is much to be said for this wholesome country environment, the quietude, the two very lovable llamas, a barbecue pit, a hot tub and sauna, a piano and a guitar, fishing and gold-panning on the creek that borders the property, a virtually untraveled road for jogging, lawn darts, a swing set, and a sandbox. A dog, two cats, croaking frogs, and a host of others (squirrels, gophers, lizards, ducks, and geese) will keep you company. A red-tailed hawk lives here; blue heron frequent the pond; and Sid, a life-sized figure of a cowboy stands guard over the hot tub. And you can not only bring the kids, you're encouraged to. Need I say more?

Guest rooms are on the lower level of the house, ideally situated for a family vacation. Each has its own private entrance, private bath, and both queen- and twin-size beds. Flora, the room that faces the garden, is papered with a deep-green raspberry-bramble pattern. Its ceiling fan revolves at a snail's pace, and the tub was especially sculpted for two. Fauna, the room I called my own, had a brass bed with a white eyelet comforter and matching pillow shams, a marble-topped table, chairs, and an armoire. The bath featured a claw-foot tub with brass fixtures and shower head. Long-range plans include two additional guest rooms upstairs.

This all-redwood ranch house, built just twenty years ago, is a showpiece of area craftsmanship. Its living room, which is open to overnight guests, is stocked with puzzles, games, and books as well as toys, musical instruments, and a stereo. An antique dental cabinet holds liqueurs for the guests' enjoyment. There is a rocking chair here, and a fireplace; oak paneling and a beamed ceiling complete the warm, homey scene.

The substantial breakfast of granola, hard-cooked eggs, bran muffins with butter, jam, and cream cheese, and a fresh-fruit platter was served family style. Beverages included coffee, tea, and freshly squeezed orange juice.

Llama pack trips may yet be in store at Llamahall Guest Ranch. Their slogan? Y'all haul with Llamahall. The company name? Pet-a-Llama Pastures.

GREEN GABLES

The CENTRAL COAST

Santa Cruz

Watsonville

17

1

101

Castroville

1

Pacific Grove
Gosby House
Green Gables
Old Monterey Inn

Salinas

68

101

Monterey

Carmel

Holiday House
Sea View Inn
Stonehouse Guest Lodge

1

Big Sur

Rose Victorian Inn

Heritage Inn

Green Gables

104 Fifth Street
Pacific Grove, California 93950; (408) 375-2095

INNKEEPERS:	*Roger and Sally Post.*
ACCOMMODATIONS:	*Six rooms, two with private bath; twin and double beds.*
RESERVATIONS:	*Six to eight weeks recommended.*
MINIMUM STAY:	*None.*
DEPOSIT:	*Full amount.*
CREDIT CARDS:	*Not accepted.*
RATES:	*Moderate to expensive.*
RESTRICTIONS:	*No pets.*

William Lacey, of the prominent Monterey Laceys, created this Queen Anne-style mansion in 1888, literally by the water's edge. A Judge Wilbur used it as a summer home in the 1890s; in this century the Gerrard family was responsible for the intelligent and systematic improvements that have kept Green Gables in mint condition. Always an impressive residence, with its wide-angle view of Monterey Bay, this relatively small but elegant dwelling has been an inn since 1958.

Roger and Sally Post were living in Pasadena when they first stayed here on a visit to the area. They told their astonished hosts that they would like nothing more than to buy it; and sure enough, when it was finally put on the market, it was to the Posts that the owners first turned. "It was one of those things that just happens," Sally says. "Call it luck — or providence."

They add that Pacific Grove has many of the advantages of a small town, but isn't isolated: the Monterey Peninsula has all the activities and attractions of any large metropolitan area. Shopping, tennis courts, boutiques, golf courses, bike paths, swimming, and the world-famous 17-Mile Drive are all close; many are within walking distance. (The good news: rooms previously available *only* during the summer months are now available year round. The Posts book a great deal of repeat business, however, so call early.)

The living room features cozy blue crumpled-velvet love seats by a fireplace, a gay carousel horse, and silk flowers. There is a pool table downstairs; in the formal dining room there is a panoramic view of the coastal shoreline. Here also there is a fireplace, and several fine Oriental rugs. Family photos grace the stairway.

The Garret Room has a gabled roof, floral wall-paper, and an iron bed with comforters; an appealing little hideaway, this. The Balcony Room has a delightful closed-in balcony with a stupendous view of the ocean. The Gable Room contains twin beds, a large desk, and blue and white wallpaper; both beds have old quilts and red bedspreads, a cheery bit of contrast that I liked.

The breakfast is Continental: homemade bread, bagels, croissants, juice, and coffee or tea served in the dining room from 7:30 to 9:30. There are fine gourmet restaurants situated in other historic homes in Pacific Grove; the Posts are more than happy to help with reservations and directions.

The Gosby House

643 Lighthouse Avenue
Pacific Grove, California 93950; (408) 375-1287

INNKEEPERS:	*Roger and Sally Post.*
ACCOMMODATIONS:	*Twenty-three rooms, twenty-one with private bath; double and queen-size beds.*
RESERVATIONS:	*One week for weekdays, four weeks for weekends.*
MINIMUM STAY:	*Two nights on weekends.*
DEPOSIT:	*Full amount.*
CREDIT CARDS:	*AE, MC, VISA.*
RATES:	*Moderate to expensive.*
RESTRICTIONS:	*No pets.*

T he Gosby House Inn, which like Green Gables is owned by Roger and Sally Post, is one of those fascinating places that have been inns right from their inception. The founder of this inn was one J. F. Gosby, an industrious native of Nova Scotia who made his way to the sunnier climes of California in 1853. He had learned the shoemaking trade at an early age and soon became the town's only cobbler. In the meantime he kept his eyes open for the main chance — which came in 1875, when the Methodist Church established religious conference grounds in a secluded area near the ocean. The shrewd Gosby, a Methodist himself, decided that an inn was needed to house the visitors and participants in the many religious and cultural activities that took place there.

So in 1887 Gosby built this comfortable, rambling inn and began almost immediately renting rooms to visitors attending the various meetings sponsored by the church. (His inn, in addition to being near the grounds, was also right across the street from the Methodist Church.) Gosby was civic-minded, gregarious, a member of many lodges, and a Town Council member from 1892 to 1896. Meanwhile the Southern Pacific railroad extended their tracks to Monterey and built the beautiful

Del Monte Hotel, also during the 1880s (building the smaller El Carmelo Hotel to handle the overflow). This brought even more visitors.

Just as the area had become firmly established as the place of choice for vacations and religious retreats, the Del Monte burned to the ground. The demand for accommodations was now overwhelming; Gosby's fortunes soared. He added a round corner tower and bay windows (late 1890s), as well as electric wiring, indoor plumbing, and connecting doors (early 1900s). In the 1920s the irrepressible cobbler changed the name of his inn to the El Carmelo Hotel, no doubt to take advantage of the more famous caravansary's name.

From 1930 onward the inn changed hands several times, finally being purchased by the present owners in 1976. It has now been rehabilitated in a manner that reflects its original glory, and is once again called by its original name. Fresh paint, brass fixtures, marble sinks, and antique furnishings throughout reflect the over twelve thousand hours necessary for restoration.

Look for the rare doll collection in the entry parlor when you arrive (and the old photograph of Mr. Gosby in front of his shoe shop). There are fresh flowers and fruit in all rooms, and complimentary tea, sherry, wine, and hors d'oeuvres in the afternoon. But the real distinction of the Gosby is in the many extras that one does not often find in a bed and breakfast. Shoes left outside your door are shined by the "Boots" (shades of an English inn); you have your choice of newspapers with breakfast, including the *Wall Street Journal* (for those who can't seem to make the total break from the financial/business world). A hall porter will arrange theater tickets and dinner reservations. Bicycles are available for riding along the Pacific Grove shoreline. (Watch for migrating gray whales from December to March, plus sea otters, pelicans, and other shore birds.)

Breakfast here is a bountiful feast sure to please every palate. Special services at the Gosby include an iron and ironing board, a sewing kit, alarm clocks, and a very thoughtful policy of celebrating special occasions such as birthdays, weddings, and anniversaries.

Old Monterey Inn

500 Martin Street
Monterey, California 93940; (408) 375-8284

INNKEEPERS:	*Ann and Gene Swett.*
ACCOMMODATIONS:	*Nine rooms and a cottage; all with private bath; twin, queen-, and king-size beds.*
RESERVATIONS:	*Two to three months for weekends.*
MINIMUM STAY:	*Two nights on weekends.*
DEPOSIT:	*In full.*
CREDIT CARDS:	*Not accepted.*
RATES:	*Expensive.*
RESTRICTIONS:	*No children. No pets.*

No doubt about it, the Old Monterey Inn is special. The only word that works here is *elegance*. And what a pleasure it is — particularly because the elegance is achieved without a hint of the ostentatious! Located in a quiet area near the heart of Monterey, the inn is surrounded by lovely gardens that create the illusion of an English country house. Architecturally it is in fact English Tudor, and owners Ann and Gene Swett have given it many of the characteristics of the finest English (and Scottish) inns.

The dwelling was built in 1929 by Carmel Martin, a former mayor and civic leader of Monterey. After passing through several hands, it was purchased and restored by the Swetts, and used exclusively as a private residence until the last of their six children flew the nest. A visit to the Sutter Creek Inn caused the Swetts to consider the possibility of creating a country-style bed and breakfast inn in the heart of Monterey. They have most definitely succeeded — to the lasting delight of the hostelry's many regular guests, including visitors to the world-famous Monterey jazz festival.

Typical of the careful architectural detail to look for at this inn are the huge timber beams and posts in the vestibule. Hand-carved designs on the stairs were done by August Gay, an artist in the community who is also responsible for the window valances.

Besides its sensational setting, it was the extras that won me over at the Old Monterey Inn. The beds aren't just beds — they're experiments in total relaxation. There are soft *and* firm pillows for each guest, and European goose down comforters. Free soft drinks and juices are stored in a refrigerator on the second floor. Breakfast is served on fine china. In the bathroom medicine cabinet I discovered the following: shampoo, nail polish remover, toothpaste, a hair dryer, a curling iron, and electric curlers. Rose petals from the garden are used to make potpourri that guests may take with them as a gift.

Branches from an old oak frame an enchanting view from the window of the Garden View room. Guests in the Library Room enjoy both a sun deck and a fireplace in this book-lined hideaway that was once actually a library. Visitors in the Dovecote room can relax by a fireplace in shadows cast by a skylight. The Cottage features a sitting room with stained glass; it also has a cozy seat in the bedroom bay window with a view of the garden.

Breakfast here is Continental, but generous — and very good. The day I was there the following was available: fresh fruit, orange juice, croissants, and whole-wheat muffins, as well as coffee, tea, and Sanka. Popovers and cheese rolls (said to be the house specialties) are served other mornings. Those who wish may have their morning meal delivered to their room or served to them in bed. On pleasant mornings breakfast is served in the garden, which provides a perfect setting for daydreaming or romancing. Complimentary wine and cheese is served every afternoon at 5:00.

The Swetts are firm believers in a quote from Boswell's *Life of Johnson:* "There is nothing which has yet been contrived by man by which so much happiness is produced as by a good tavern or inn." This is one of those rare places that delivers this total serenity and pleasure. It is also one of the few that must be experienced to be believed.

Sea View Inn

Camino Real between Eleventh and Twelfth, P.O. Box 4138
Carmel, California 93921; (408) 624-8778

INNKEEPERS:	*Marshall and Diane Hydorn.*
ACCOMMODATIONS:	*Eight rooms, six with private bath; twin, queen-, and king-size beds.*
RESERVATIONS:	*Three weeks recommended.*
MINIMUM STAY:	*Two nights on holidays and weekends.*
DEPOSIT:	*First night's lodging.*
CREDIT CARDS:	*MC, VISA.*
RATES:	*Inexpensive to moderate.*
RESTRICTIONS:	*No children under twelve. No pets.*

Here's an economical bed and breakfast where one can park the car and take it from there on foot. (It's three blocks from the beach; five from Ocean Avenue, Carmel's main street.) This country-style Victorian, built in 1906, is one of the oldest guest houses in this artists'-colony-by-the-sea. Yet it is well out of the tourist crush; located in a residential neighborhood, there is no traffic noise or other distractions associated with congested downtown areas.

The Sea View is popular as a honeymoon haven; don't be surprised if you meet guests returning for their anniversaries. (One couple who had spent their wedding night here fifty years ago returned recently on their fiftieth anniversary.) It is also patronized regularly by visitors to the jazz and Bach festivals, both annual events in Monterey and Carmel, respectively. (Book a room early if you are attending either; accommodations are hard to get during the festivals.)

Proprietors Marshall and Diane Hydorn first visited Carmel looking for a vacation house. (Marshall was flying for TWA and Diane was occupied as a homemaker, raising the couple's children.) More as a joke than anything else, they asked the real estate agent if there were any "little inns" for sale. "As a matter of fact, there is one," was the sobering reply. The Hydorns were hooked as soon as they saw it.

This is an adult hideaway where privacy is everything, but children over twelve are allowed as long as they are reasonably well-behaved. The Sea View is furnished with antiques blended in with newer pieces; a great many belongings of the hosts are to be found around the house, too, adding to the personal feeling of the inn. The Hydorns try to give their guests as much attention as possible. They are well informed about local happenings and attractions, including good local restaurants.

The Continental breakfast is served in the living room, before the fireplace, and varies from day to day. When I visited there were assorted cold cereals, juice, fresh fruit, whole-grain toast, and muffins. (And, of course, a choice of hot drinks: tea, coffee, herb tea, and cocoa.) A tasty coffee cake is served other mornings, and on certain Sundays Diane has been known to make quiche as a special treat. Complimentary sherry is served in the afternoon.

Holiday House

Camino Real at Seventh, P.O. Box 782
Carmel, California 93921; (408) 624-6267

INNKEEPERS:	*Dieter and Ruth Back.*
ACCOMMODATIONS:	*Six rooms, four with private bath; twin, double, and queen-size beds.*
RESERVATIONS:	*Eight weeks for weekends.*
MINIMUM STAY:	*Two nights on weekends.*
DEPOSIT:	*First night's lodging.*
CREDIT CARDS:	*Not accepted.*
RATES:	*Moderate.*
RESTRICTIONS:	*No infants. No pets.*

A few years ago Dieter and Ruth Back found themselves stopping over in Carmel frequently on trips between Los Angeles and San Francisco. Eventually this amiable couple moved to the Monterey Peninsula, and when they heard that Holiday House was up for sale they thought they'd give the bed and breakfast business a try. The Backs were not total strangers to the accommodations trade, however. They owned and managed apartment houses in Los Angeles and already operated the Acacia Lodge in Carmel Valley. "What we like about bed and breakfast is that it offers a more personal experience — the chance to meet people and get to know them," Dieter told me as we walked the beautifully landscaped lawns of Holiday House.

This brown-shingled dwelling was built in 1905 by a Stanford University professor as a family summer home — and also as a retreat for students and faculty. The living room and sun porch (both of which are open to guests) have a marvelous ocean view and a stone fireplace. Books and games are available. There are also gardens for guests to enjoy: all of the six bedrooms look out to sea, or onto a garden. The house is perfectly located; it's a five minutes' walk to the beach or to village shops, galleries, and a wide variety of restaurants.

Holiday House has been furnished with antiques and collectibles, most purchased locally. There is no TV or swimming pool here; the Backs feel that such conveniences defeat the objective of a bed and breakfast inn, which is rest and relaxation. There is a small pond on the grounds, with a terrace and a stone bench, which adds to the introspective mood of the place. Not that it is without whimsy: all rooms have fresh flowers, but are also stocked with a full supply of jellybeans! Some rooms are directly under the sloping roof, which imparts a cozy, hidden-away feeling. Most are furnished in decor appropriate to the turn of the century; some of the art work is by local artists.

The Point Lobos room features a fine view of Point Lobos and has a queen-size bed. Rustic paneling, decorative shades, and blue, red, and beige patterns on both wallpaper and bedspread set an upbeat mood. Terrace South, with its private back entrance, offers a queen and a twin bed — perfect for a family of three or as a third-party set-up.

A hearty breakfast is served buffet style between 8:30 and 9:30, in the dining room or on the sun porch. There is a selection of cold cereals, coffee cake, and English muffins (occasionally bagels with cream cheese), a quiche or a ham and cheese casserole, fresh fruit, and coffee, tea, and orange juice.

Since Holiday House has been a guest house since the 1920s, staying here has become a family tradition with some guests. Its pronounced order and cleanliness, its relaxing atmosphere, and its reasonable rates all make it a real find — particularly for those who must watch their budgets, but still wish to avoid the impersonality of the big hotels and faceless motels that have proliferated in the area.

Stonehouse Inn

Monte Verde and Eighth, P.O. Box 2517
Carmel, California 93921; (408) 624-4569

INNKEEPER:	*Virginia Carey.*
ACCOMMODATIONS:	*Six rooms, all with shared bath; double and king-size beds.*
RESERVATIONS:	*Four to six weeks for weekends.*
MINIMUM STAY:	*None.*
DEPOSIT:	*Full amount.*
CREDIT CARDS:	*MC, VISA.*
RATES:	*Expensive.*
RESTRICTIONS:	*No children under fourteen. No pets.*

Stonehouse was built in 1906 by Josephine Foster, Carmel's resident bohemian. She was a great friend of the arts — of writers particularly — and among her guests were the brightest literary lights of her time: Jack London, Sinclair Lewis, Mary Austin, poet George Sterling. (In those days one didn't have to write, drink, or throw wild parties to be considered bohemian — all one had to do was be a patron of the arts.) Josephine was known affectionately as "Nana" by her friends, of whom there were many on the Monterey Peninsula.

Nana's family was artistic. Her grandfather built the first Cliff House in San Francisco (destroyed later by fire). Stonehouse reflects her idiosyncratic taste. All the stones are carefully arranged and mortared together in the manner of the stone houses of Pennsylvania; creeping vines cover its exterior. Records show that the stones were hand shaped by local Indian craftsmen, and the unique star-shaped window in the front of the dwelling may have been fashioned by one of these men.

Stonehouse is furnished with country-flavored antiques throughout. The living room features a large stone fireplace (sherry, wine, and hot cider are served to guests here before they leave for dinner in the evenings). All guest rooms have handmade quilts, silk flower arrangements, fluffy pillows, and complimentary fresh fruit.

The bedrooms are named after authors. The one named after George Sterling (it was he who wrote that San Francisco was a "cool gray city of love") contains a handsome king-size canopy bed with a floral comforter, a dust ruffle, and pillow shams. There's an antique dresser, and a comfortable rocking chair and a reading lamp for quiet moments with a book. The Jack London room has an antique armoire and a queen-size bed with a wrought-iron and brass frame, as well as a single bed. Both rooms have good views of Point Lobos.

My favorite room was the Sinclair Lewis. Large and airy, with a huge brass bed, this room's big windows overlooking the rooftop and trees reminded me of the rooms at my grandmother's house when I was a very small child.

The full breakfast includes a hot entrée (baked eggs with bacon, crustless quiche, seafood crêpes), fresh fruit, homemade muffins, juice, and coffee. Breakfast is served from 8:30 to 10:00 A.M., and guests may eat either in the dining room, or — in good weather — on the patio.

One interesting legend about Stonehouse: Nana Foster is reputed to have placed "important papers" within the stone walls on the left-hand side of the fireplace. Writings by her accomplished literary friends? Some of her own literary efforts, perhaps? We may never know. No one's been able to tear the fireplace apart to find out — it's too beautiful."

Heritage Inn

978 Olive Street
San Luis Obispo, California 93401; (805) 544-7440

INNKEEPERS:	*Jim and Zella Harrison.*
ACCOMMODATIONS:	*Nine rooms, one with private bath; twin, double, and queen-size beds.*
RESERVATIONS:	*Three weeks recommended.*
MINIMUM STAY:	*None.*
DEPOSIT:	*Full amount.*
CREDIT CARDS:	*MC, VISA.*
RATES:	*Moderate.*
RESTRICTIONS:	*No children. No pets.*

The history of the Heritage Inn in San Luis Obispo sounds more like the Perils of Pauline than the usual guidebook fare. The saga began in 1902, when the San Luis Obispo Herrera family (one of the old Hispanic families in the area) built this gracious three-thousand-square-foot home as a family dwelling. As its ten bedrooms would indicate, the Herreras were a large family: Manuel was the city's constable, Isbaldo the custodian at the courthouse; Juanita, the oldest daughter, worked for the Tribune Printing Company. About 1930 the residence was sold to Frank Barcellos, a local saloon owner who moved it from Monterey Street (then the intersection of Highways 1 and 101) to Santa Rosa Street and used it as a lodging establishment for men.

In January 1981 the building was bought by Rob and Kathy Strong, who hoped to renovate it and use it as a bed and breakfast inn. The condition of the sale was that the Strongs move the structure to another location to make way for a parking lot. The couple scheduled the house's dramatic half-mile move, only to be halted at the last moment by a neighboring motel's protest. Some frantic legal maneuvering followed — capped by the court's decision that the Heritage Inn could be moved, just hours before the wrecker's ball would have demolished it forever.

An interesting sidelight: the inn's new location was purchased from another branch of the Herrera family. And where was this new creekside location for Heritage Inn? Once again at the intersection of Highways 1 and 101.

I'm glad the good guys won this round, because this is not just the only bed and breakfast in San Luis Obispo, it is a quality establishment by any standard. Current owners Jim and Zella Harrison maintain the precedents set by the Strongs that make this a success.

The character of the inn is turn of the century: antique furnishings (most from the area), period wall coverings and draperies, bay windows and window seats throughout, period bath fixtures, and a wide and well-chosen variety of San Luis Obispo memorabilia and photos. Guest rooms are provided with brass, wicker, and oak antiques; fresh flowers; and washbasins.

A Continental breakfast is served in the fireside dining room: croissants, muffins, and nut breads, homemade spreads, fresh fruit in season, juice, coffee, or tea.

The reception room provides a large variety of local tourist information and a menu selection from local restaurants (Heritage hostesses are quite eager to help here also); wine and cheese are served in the parlor in the evening; bubble bath is available in the bathrooms; parking is easy — just a few of the reasons people from San Francisco, Los Angeles, and the San Joaquin Valley are finding Heritage Inn the ideal mid-coast stop during that long drive down El Camino Real.

Rose Victorian Inn

789 Valley Road
Arroyo Grande, California 93420; (805) 481-5566

INNKEEPERS:	Diane and Ross Cox.
ACCOMMODATIONS:	Six rooms, one with private bath; twin, double, queen-, and king-size beds.
RESERVATIONS:	Three weeks recommended.
MINIMUM STAY:	Two nights on holiday weekends.
DEPOSIT:	Full amount.
CREDIT CARDS:	AE, MC, VISA (to reserve a room only if there's not time enough to send a check).
RATES:	Expensive.
RESTRICTIONS:	Children: Minimum age sixteen. No pets.

hen people ask me what it takes to be an innkeeper," explained Diane Cox, "I ask *them* if they like a Grand Central Station lifestyle, and can function on just six hours of sleep.

Diane was born in China of mixed English and American parentage. Her family migrated to the United States and resided in Laguna Beach through the 1940s and fifties. This is where she met husband Ross. "We met in first grade, dated in high school, married in college, and have been living that Grand Central Station lifestyle I mentioned ever since — Ross has forty-one cousins, I have almost as many."

Their inn is a family affair. Ross is a builder by trade. Son-in-law John is the landscape architect who drew up the plans for the six-acre property. Daughter Shelly serves as part-time innkeeper, and another daughter is responsible for much of the interior design of the inn.

The Rose Victorian is truly classified as a country inn, due to its adjoining restaurant/bar operation. The purchase of overnight accommodations on the modified

American plan includes breakfast (a fresh fruit plate, home-baked muffins, eggs Florentine, orange juice with champagne) *and* dinner.

This fourteen-room house, once the homestead of a large walnut farm, is a classic example of Victorian Italian/Stick architecture, with vertical lines predominating. It is painted in four shades of rose, following the Victorian tradition of picking a color and then painting the house in several shades of that color. Original coal-burning fireplaces heat the living room and parlor.

The six bed and breakfast rooms for overnight guests are filled with mahogany, oak, rosewood, and walnut pieces that carry out the Victorian decor. Each room is named after a variety of rose and decorated in its color: Sterling Silver, Tropicana, Olé, Brandy, Summer Sunshine. A vase with a rose of the same name, from the over two hundred rose bushes planted on the property, is found in each room.

Celebrities, writers, movie producers, and occasionally government officials come here to stay. And, as Shelly aptly pointed out, that is one of the unique features of the Rose Victorian: once you've arrived there's no need to go anywhere else. You can play croquet on the lawn, sip iced tea and nibble on hors d'oeuvres in the late afternoon, feast on sumptuous Steak au Poivre, Roast Duck à l'Orange, or Shrimp Victoria, enjoy an after-dinner drink, relax in your room, or mingle with the other guests in the parlor or living room around the grand piano.

But then again it would be a shame *not* to go out, as the area has so many attractions: the Great American Melodrama and Vaudeville Show in neighboring Oceano; boating, fishing, and windsurfing at Lopez Lake; mineral hot springs; wineries and Spanish missions. It's a forty-five minute drive north to Hearst Castle; San Luis Obispo is just fifteen minutes away.

SEAL BEACH INN

SOUTHERN CALIFORNIA

San Luis Obispo

101

Los Alamos
Union Hotel

Bath Street Inn
Glenborough Inn
Old Yacht Club Inn
The Parsonage

Santa Barbara

Oxnard

101

La Maida
The Venice Beach House

Los Angeles

Long Beach

Seal Beach

Laguna Beach

Carlsbad

San Diego

Seal Beach Inn
The Carriage House

Eiler's Inn

Riverside

Rock Haus

Britt House

101 5 10 15 78 8 1

Union Hotel

362 Bell Street
Los Alamos, California 93440; (805) 344-2744

INNKEEPERS:	*Dick and Teri Langdon.*
ACCOMMODATIONS:	*Fourteen rooms, three with private bath; twin and double beds.*
RESERVATIONS:	*Three to six weeks recommended.*
MINIMUM STAY:	*None.*
DEPOSIT:	*In full.*
CREDIT CARDS:	*Not accepted.*
RATES:	*Moderate to expensive.*
RESTRICTIONS:	*No children. No pets.*

J. D. Snyder was a New Yorker who came west to make his fortune — and succeeded. In the 1880s he owned the way station in tiny Los Alamos for the stagecoach route between Santa Barbara and San Francisco. In addition to being the local agent for Wells Fargo, he was also involved in farming and a variety of other business ventures in Santa Barbara County. One of them was the Union Hotel, where stage passengers could eat, stay overnight, and wet their whistles before continuing the arduous overland journey.

Fire destroyed the hotel, however, as it did so many other wooden structures of that time. In 1915 it was rebuilt with Indian adobe. Thereafter it was used as a hotel, a rooming house, and a pool room, after which it was boarded up and forgotten. Until it was discovered by Dick Langdon, that is. It became his dream to rehabilitate — or rather *re-create* — this old western hotel based on original sketches of the Union. Wood from twelve barns was used to recreate the exterior; various craftspeople in the area contributed their talents. The result is a work of art that has attracted comment from western buffs and bed and breakfast enthusiasts alike.

Antiques here are imaginative and provocative: two-hundred-year-old Egyptian urns; a pair of swinging doors from a New Orleans house of ill repute; dining room furniture from a Mississippi plantation; an 1880 Brunswick pool table. My room was a masterpiece of whimsy: a ceiling fan, an antique trunk, hats hanging from a coatrack! (I kept waiting for the owners of those hats to come back and claim them.) There is an old crank telephone in the upstairs hall, and guests who listen carefully to the earphone are often surprised by mysterious (taped) voices.

Overnight guests dine together at 7:30 P.M. — children are charged by their weight. Then everyone gathers in the old saloon for authentic ghost stories, an evening's worth of entertainment (sometimes Dick plays tapes from his collection of old radio shows), popcorn and wine.

One of the most interesting architectural and designing triumphs of this inn is the swimming pool. There were no such conveniences in the 1880s, so Dick concealed this one in the guise of an old-fashioned reflecting pool. The grounds also include streetlights, park benches, flower gardens, and manicured lawns. There is a lovely Victorian gazebo with a secret Jacuzzi inside (raised hydraulically at night), large enough to accommodate a dozen guests.

A full breakfast is served, and it is as special as everything else about the place. It has been known to include such diverse delights as gingerbread cake, chocolate chip cookies, pound cake, and brandy. After breakfast guests are treated to a tour of Los Alamos in a 1918, fifteen-passenger touring car.

This distinctive adventure in lodging is only open on Friday, Saturday, and Sunday (all year round). "Three days a week is fun," Dick is often quoted as saying. "After that, it becomes work." Be sure to book early — word of mouth has made the Union Hotel one of the most popular attractions in the area.

The Old Yacht Club Inn

431 Corona Del Mar
Santa Barbara, California 93103; (805) 962-1277

INNKEEPER:	*Nancy Donaldson.*
ACCOMMODATIONS:	*Five rooms, one with private bath; queen-size beds.*
RESERVATIONS:	*Two to three months for weekends.*
MINIMUM STAY:	*Two nights on weekends.*
DEPOSIT:	*First night's lodging.*
CREDIT CARDS:	*AE, MC, VISA.*
RATES:	*Moderate to expensive.*
RESTRICTIONS:	*No children. No pets.*

T ake four independent career women. Add a historic structure crying out for tender loving care. Stir in a need to try something new and different, and you have the highly successful ingredients of one of Santa Barbara's most comfortable bed and breakfast inns.

The Old Yacht Club Inn was built in 1912 as a private residence on Cabrillo Boulevard overlooking the beautiful Pacific. In the 1920s Santa Barbara's yacht club was completely destroyed by a disastrous storm. The present structure was pressed into service as the headquarters for the club; later it was moved to its current location on Corona Del Mar.

Nancy Donaldson, the dean of a Los Angeles high school, and three female friends — also educators and administrators — cooperated to buy, renovate, furnish, and finally operate the Old Yacht Club Inn. Just a short distance from lovely Cabrillo Beach, the OYCI has five tastefully decorated guest rooms.

Although all share baths, rooms come with washbasins; there is a small decanter at bedside for guests whose slumber is improved by a sip or two of sherry. The two front rooms have balconies surrounded by flowers.

wood floors, a window seat, bedspread and drapes with a brightly colored flower print. (I also liked the Portofino room, with its baby blues and tan and cream.) All rooms are decorated with antiques, and the front rooms catch the sun and a delicious afternoon breeze.

Guests are invited to share the living room area as well as the spacious front porch. (Arriving guests are given a glass of wine or a cup of tea in the living room.) There is a fireplace here, but no TV. As a native of the area, Nancy is well equipped to steer guests to the best restaurants and nearby attractions. Bicycles are available to guests, as are beach chairs and towels. Guests who arrive on Amtrak or at the airport can be picked up.

The breakfast is fuller than most, usually featuring egg dishes, with fresh fruit, juice, homemade breads (zucchini and banana), and coffee cake. Nancy will also cook dinner for guests who request it in advance (mainly on weekends). Request it — she's an *excellent* cook!

Postscript: I just received word that the innkeepers of the Old Yacht Club Inn have opened the Hitchcock House (next door): four new rooms, all with private entrances and private baths. Each was decorated by a different partner, in keeping with the family tradition.

Bath Street Inn

1720 Bath Street
Santa Barbara, California 93101; (805) 682-9680

INNKEEPERS:	*Susan Brown and Nancy Stover.*
ACCOMMODATIONS:	*Seven rooms, all with private bath; twin, queen-, and king-size beds.*
RESERVATIONS:	*Six weeks recommended.*
MINIMUM STAY:	*Two nights on weekends.*
DEPOSIT:	*Half the full amount.*
CREDIT CARDS:	*MC, VISA.*
RATES:	*Moderate.*
RESTRICTIONS:	*No children. No pets.*

From the time Vizcaíno entered the harbor on the eve of Saint Barbara's Day in 1602 (and so, appropriately, named the channel for her), Santa Barbara has been a magnet for adventurers, visionaries, entrepreneurs, and most of all people irresistibly attracted to its mild climate and scenic beauty. Both newcomers and old Santa Barbara hands have found the Bath Street Inn ideally located for maximum enjoyment of the city's rich cultural and resort activities.

Bath Street Inn began as a private residence in 1895, and was called the House of the Three Sisters by local residents. (At least partly because of the huge *Pittosporum* tree with three trunks that stood outside, it would seem.) When Susan Brown found it with the aid of a realtor, the old dwelling was badly in need of some sisterly attention. And it got it — with the help of a local architect who did much of the renovation.

A common theme among owners of bed and breakfast inns is a desire to leave an environment of cutthroat ambition and enter a service-oriented world. Susan — a personnel manager in Anaheim for ten years — was no exception. This charming and intelligent woman pronounced herself "somewhat disillusioned with the business world." Or at least its most competitive and least reflective aspects.

At the same time, she offers a service that businesses of all descriptions find eminently helpful: seminar facilities and a conference room.

This Queen Anne Victorian has three stories with a small second-story eyelid balcony in front, and is larger inside than it appears from the street. (The third floor — where the common area is located — feels like an entire house in itself.) The rooms are decorated with a nice mix of antiques that combine the 1895 atmosphere of the original dwelling.

The Continental breakfast is served outdoors on the porch or patio when weather permits — which it usually does in Santa Barbara. It consists of homemade breads, rolls, coffee cake or croissants, juice, fresh fruit in season, and a choice of coffee, tea, milk, or cocoa.

The Glenborough Inn

1327 Bath Street
Santa Barbara, California 93101; (805) 966-0589

INNKEEPERS:	*Jo Ann Bell and Pat Hardy.*
ACCOMMODATIONS:	*Eight rooms, four with private bath; double and queen-size beds.*
RESERVATIONS:	*Two to three months for weekends.*
MINIMUM STAY:	*Two nights on weekends.*
DEPOSIT:	*Full amount.*
CREDIT CARDS:	*MC, VISA.*
RATES:	*Moderate to expensive.*
RESTRICTIONS:	*Children under 12 discouraged. Pets discouraged.*

T he Glenborough is a handsome, two-story structure built in 1906 in what is often termed the California Craftsman style. Built by a single craftsman for Louis Brooks, vice president of a local fuel company, it was quite modern for its time, with a decorative brass heater instead of the traditional wood fireplace. But in renovating, decoration and design has mainly followed the turn-of-the-century mode of the architecture. With few exceptions, furnishings are antiques — even the curtains are of old lace or crochet. Rooms have pictures from the early 1900s, and a very special part of the decor are the Fillmore-signed nostalgic L.A. prints.

Proprietors Jo Ann Bell and Pat Hardy met when they served together on the board of directors of a battered women's shelter in Riverside. Jo Ann has a background in social work as a psychotherapist, and still maintains a small practice. Pat is a former director of a crisis hotline, a people-oriented bundle of creative energy whom Jo Ann describes as a "greeter, a morning person, and a risk-taker." The decorating was done mainly by Pat, with Jo Ann "keeping things from getting outrageous."

The French Rose room is graced by elegant inlaid French furniture and a rose velvet spread; my favorite of all four rooms in the main house, this spacious chamber has a fine mountain view framed by antique embroidered curtains. Aurelia's Fancy celebrates a young woman who once lived here, with a rocking chair, a full queen-size cannonball field bed accented with rich blue, antique lace curtains and an heirloom quilt. The Country room projects a cozy ambience, its earthy tones enlivened by the morning sun, with antique golden oak furniture. The Garden room is the smallest but cheeriest, a former sun porch overlooking a garden, with an antique brass and white iron double bed; furniture is wicker and antique oak, accented by lush plants.

Four of the Glenborough's eight guest rooms are in an early 1880s cottage across the street, with separate entrances, a secluded New Orleans—style garden, and a private bath for each room.

Wine, tea, and hors d'oeuvres are served in a pleasant parlor in the evening; there is a hot tub in the garden that may be reserved for private use.

Breakfast at the Glenborough was delicious. A platter of fresh fruit (baked apple in wintertime); homemade coffee cake and nut breads (pumpkin and banana); Moma's egg casserole; orange, cranberry, or apple juice; and tea, cinnamon-laced coffee, or cocoa. The morning meal is served between 8:00 and 9:30, and is served to guests in their rooms — in bed if desired.

"We don't necessarily emphasize a homey atmosphere that much," says Pat. "We believe many of our guests come here for privacy."

The Parsonage

1600 Olive Street
Santa Barbara, California 93101; (805) 962-9336

INNKEEPER:	*Hilde Michelmore.*
ACCOMMODATIONS:	*Five rooms, all with private bath; queen- and king-size beds.*
RESERVATIONS:	*Two to six weeks recommended.*
MINIMUM STAY:	*Two nights on weekends.*
DEPOSIT:	*First night's lodging.*
CREDIT CARDS:	*MC, VISA.*
RATES:	*Moderate to expensive.*
RESTRICTIONS:	*No children under fourteen. No pets.*

I f you need some tender loving care, plan to spend a day or two with Hilde Michelmore at The Parsonage. "TLC" is Hilde's specialty, and perhaps it was the similar orientation of the former residents that drew her to this house, once a parsonage for the Trinity Episcopal Church. "I just loved the house when I first saw it," she says of this Queen Anne Victorian built in 1892. "I looked at it one month, and moved in the next."

The Parsonage is now very much a home for Hilde, and a home away from home for her guests, many of whom find such an instant rapport with her that they invite her out to dinner. From the TV in the living room to the generous, but informal breakfast served on the sun deck (cheese soufflé, apple-bran muffins, a slice of watermelon, coffee, and juice), you find the owner/operator school of philosophy. As Hilde insists, "When you lose that, you lose the whole concept of what bed and breakfast is all about."

The house sits on the corner of Olive and Arrellaga streets on Santa Barbara's upper east side. A wrought-iron gate leads to the large front porch that invites you into the high-ceilinged parlor and library, once used for church business. Redwood moldings are in evidence, as is a bird's-eye redwood fireplace. Hilde has incorporated her personal furnishings with pieces she purchased especially for the house.

Each guest room has its own bathroom, although some are larger than others and one or two are closet size. The Rosebud Room is the only downstairs bedroom and unfortunately I didn't get to see it, as it was occupied at the time. Of the four upstairs rooms, however, I can highly recommend the Honeymoon Suite, which runs the entire length of the front of the house, with one gorgeous view of the ocean, palm trees, and the downtown area. The suite consists of a bedroom with a king-size canopied bed and an antique armoire, a bath (with a marble-topped washstand and a pedestal sink), and a solarium with an abundance of light filtering through its many clear and stained-glass windows. The other rooms, Lavender and Lace, Las Flores, and the Peacock Room, carry out the various themes suggested by their names.

Santa Barbara's lovely beaches, botanical gardens, golf courses, art galleries, and fine restaurants make for a great L.A. get-away weekend or an unhurried stopover before heading south to the City of the Angels.

La Maida House

11159 La Maida Street
North Hollywood, California 91601; (818) 769-3857

INNKEEPER:	*Megan Timothy.*
ACCOMMODATIONS:	*Nine rooms, all with private bath; twin, double, queen-, and king-size beds.*
RESERVATIONS:	*Three weeks recommended.*
MINIMUM STAY:	*Two nights on weekends.*
DEPOSIT:	*First night's lodging.*
CREDIT CARDS:	*Not accepted.*
RATES:	*Moderate to expensive.*
RESTRICTIONS:	*No children. No pets.*

A ll the great things you've been hearing about La Maida House are true. This twenty-five-room, seven-thousand-square-foot Italian villa is the crème de la crème of the small inns. Its marble fireplace, spiral staircase, French doors, beveled glass mirrors, and bubbling fountains are reminiscent of the glamorous Hollywood of the thirties and forties. The house was actually built in 1926 by one T.G. La Maida, a fruit and vegetable rancher. The largest guest room, Cipresso, overlooks the cypress trees along La Maida Street. Its canopied bed, ceiling fan, and wicker furniture remind one of warmer climes—perhaps Zimbabwe, which is where innkeeper Megan Timothy hails from.

Other touches I like here: AM/FM clock radios in the guest rooms, down comforters and wool blankets, a copy of the *Los Angeles Times* delivered to the door, bathroom scales for the weight-conscious, full laundry and dry-cleaning service on request—and Megan will even prepare lunch or dinner for a tired and weary traveler with a little advance notice.

"Our guests are guests in the true sense of the word," said Megan. "In Africa when we had house guests we catered to their every little whim. That's what I'm striving to re-create here."

A woman of many talents, this Megan. A caterer by profession, a patron of the arts, a sculptor in stained-glass, a photographer extraordinaire, an interior designer, and even a one-time professional folk singer.

Everything here is homemade, right down to the blended yogurt–fruit juice beverages served at breakfast and the *padkos* (an African tradition of food for the road) Megan gives guests as a parting gift. What for many other innkeepers is the lull in their day, is for Megan the busiest part; she was baking oatmeal cookies when I arrived in the early afternoon. Megan keeps chickens for fresh eggs, grows her own fruits, vegetables and herbs, and makes her own jams and preserves.

Writers, producers, directors, and celebrities are entered on La Maida's guest list. Part of the reason is that the inn is so close to most of the major studios (Universal, Burbank, Columbia, Warner Brothers, NBC). La Maida has even seen a little movie-making of its own. The house was featured in scenes of "Quincy" and the popular TV series "Simon and Simon."

Other nearby attractions include the Hollywood Bowl (Megan will provide a picnic basket or pre-concert supper), the Huntington Library and gardens, the Norton Simon Museum, and the L.A. County Museum. (La Maida is a quick ten minutes from the Hollywood/Burbank airport.)

Speaking of art, Megan's breakfast is a feast of edible art. The fare includes freshly baked breads (scones, brioches, or oatmeal muffins), an attractive carved-fruit platter with Tunisian oranges (sprinkled with rosewater and cinnamon), and a refreshing fresh fruit/yogurt drink such as peach-rosewater-honey or mint-pepper. (Bing cherries partially dipped in bittersweet chocolate were served at bedside.)

So the question is: Is it Hollywood, or Zimbabwe? Perhaps it's the best of both.

The Venice Beach House

15 Thirtieth Avenue
Venice, California 90291; (213) 823-1966

INNKEEPERS:	*Philip and Vivian Boesch.*
ACCOMMODATIONS:	*Eight rooms, four with private bath; double, queen-, and king-size beds.*
RESERVATIONS:	*Two weeks recommended.*
MINIMUM STAY:	*Two nights on weekends.*
DEPOSIT:	*Half total amount.*
CREDIT CARDS:	*AE, MC, VISA.*
RATES:	*Moderate to expensive.*
RESTRICTIONS:	*No children under ten. No pets.*

Abbot Kinney made his fortune in the thriving tobacco industry of his day. Around the turn of the century he bought up some marshland on the coast of California near Los Angeles, and in an attempt to re-create Venice, Italy, he constructed piers, boardwalks, bathhouses, and canals. Kinney was called a dreamer by some, but his project (dubbed "Kinney's Folly") soon brought the rich and famous to his door. Venice experienced its heyday as a resort town through the early 1900s. Then a series of disasters and misfortunes started it on a long, slow decline.

Today Venice is as much a state of mind as anything else. People either love it, or shun it — there's nothing in between. Most of the action is found on the beach boardwalk, where vendors ply their wares in an open-air market, punk rockers on roller skates command one's attention, and muscle men strut their stuff.

If you're one of those who love it (or are perhaps just a bit curious), then you'll adore the Venice Beach House, a California bungalow-style bed and breakfast inn opened just two years ago by Philip and Vivian Boesch. Needless to say, this perky young couple love this zany beach town, and they've made it their home for the past seven years. Philip is a communications industry attorney;

Vivian a Louisiana transplant who should be properly thanked for bringing Southern hospitality to southern California.

The inn's guest rooms remember Kinney's Venice of America in both name and decor. Warren Wilson's Room commemorates the newspaperman who built this retreat in 1911. Tramp's Quarters honors Charlie Chaplin, the original Venice tramp who created his famous character here in the film *Kid Auto Races at Venice Beach.* Of course there's Abbot Kinney's Room and the Pier Suite. Finally, there is James Peasgood's Room, lest we forget this rascal who changed the history of Venice forever by embezzling the city treasury in 1922.

A light Continental breakfast of fresh fruit, muffins, coffee, and juice is served from 8:00 to 10:00; wine and cheese from 5:30 to 7:00. Gourmet picnic lunches are available on request.

Washington Street's shops and sidewalk cafes are just a block away, as is the beach itself. The inn provides bicycles and beach chairs. In quiet moments you can curl up by the fire in the spacious living room with its beamed ceiling and bay windows, or sit out on the patio with a glass of sun tea and read the inn's copy of the colorful history of Venice, *Venice California 1904–1930,* by Jeffrey Stanton.

Venice has been most recently described as "a city that's striving to make a comeback." I applaud Philip and Vivian Boesch, who are certainly doing their part to help.

The Seal Beach Inn

212 Fifth Street
Seal Beach, California 90740; (213) 430-3915

INNKEEPERS:	*Marjorie and Jack Bettenhausen.*
ACCOMMODATIONS:	*Twenty-four rooms, all with private bath; twin, double, queen-, and king-size beds.*
RESERVATIONS:	*Two weeks recommended.*
MINIMUM STAY:	*Two nights on weekends.*
DEPOSIT:	*First night's lodging.*
CREDIT CARDS:	*AE, MC, VISA.*
RATES:	*Moderate to expensive.*
RESTRICTIONS:	*Children discouraged. No pets.*

T he Spanish called it Rancho Los Alamitos; the German burghers who followed knew it as Anaheim Landing. Bay City was the rather slick monicker cooked up by developers in the 1920s. Today this sleepy coastal village is known as Seal Beach (after the many seals that once flocked to the beaches here), but it is in many ways just as quiet now as it was in former days — which for those of us who wish to get away from it all is a big plus. Yet the nearby convergence of three major freeways make Los Angeles and destinations in Orange County easy to get to when it's time to get back to the real world.

The style of The Seal Beach Inn is French Mediterranean, a perfect choice for this part of the state. When one first hears of its twenty-two rooms, one imagines that this might be a motel that serves breakfast. Not a bit of it! The rooms are equipped with antiques and warm, quality furnishings, carefully designed to impart a Continental country inn flavor. (All rooms have private baths, and kitchen-bars are available in most.) Prints, objets d'art, collectibles, and books abound in most rooms. There is a pool, as one might expect in southern California; and there is also an attractive garden with roses, geraniums, hibiscus, and begonias (among other flowers).

Seal Beach Inn began as a motel in the 1920s, when Seal Beach was a wide-open gambling and resort area, which makes the European feeling of this place all the more remarkable. ("The closest thing to Europe since I left there," reads one encomium in the register.) Hardwood floors and wood paneling are everywhere. Antique lamp posts and a brick courtyard, blue awnings and a yellow-painted fence, and an ancient British telephone booth all add to the ambience.

Proprietors Marjorie Bettenhausen and physician husband Jack go out of their way to provide those little extras that make a bed and breakfast different from any other kind of accommodation. Current magazines and the *Los Angeles Times* are available in the breakfast room; there are laundry facilities for the use of guests (including an ironing board). Just one block from the ocean, Seal Beach Inn is also close to the Old Town section of Seal Beach (the high percentage of artists and craftspeople living in the area is obvious in the boutiques and shops), the Long Beach marina, and a total of four shopping areas on various waterfronts. (And the inn is just fifteen to twenty minutes by car from the *Queen Mary,* Knott's Berry Farm, and Disneyland.)

Breakfast in the breakfast room begins at 7:30 and lasts until 10:30. French and American pastries, marmalade and butter, freshly squeezed orange juice, and coffee and tea are all served buffet style — although one can have them brought to the room on request.

Marjorie and Jack enjoy what they do, as becomes obvious when one talks to them about their work. "Every day it's something different," Marjorie told me. One interesting moment came when two attractive French girls admitted sadly that they had run out of money. What to do? Before a call could be placed to the French Embassy, two French pilots checked in, and *voila!* . . . the next day the two young women were flown back to Paris free of charge. A charming story, and one that might have an interesting follow-up . . .

Eiler's Inn

741 South Coast Highway
Laguna Beach, California 92651; (714) 494-3004

INNKEEPERS:	*Henk and Annette Wirtz.*
ACCOMMODATIONS:	*Twelve rooms, all with private bath; twin, double, queen-, and king-size beds.*
RESERVATIONS:	*Four to five weeks recommended.*
MINIMUM STAY:	*Two nights on weekends.*
DEPOSIT:	*First two nights' lodging.*
CREDIT CARDS:	*AE, MC, VISA.*
RATES:	*Expensive.*
RESTRICTIONS:	*Children discouraged. No pets.*

Eiler Larsen was a Danish immigrant with a passion for wishing people well — an agreeable eccentricity (if eccentricity it really is) that made him a well-loved local figure in Laguna Beach. The colorful Dane simply loved to say hello to people, and each day strode up and down Laguna Beach greeting residents and strangers alike. In the 1960s he was made the town's official greeter by the municipal government, and as the irrepressible old gentleman grew older and declined in health, the tabs for his meals and lodging were quietly picked up by government and business people. When he passed away in 1975, he left a warm memory of a man who represented perhaps the highest form of hospitality: a desire to make others feel good with no reward for oneself except the company of one's friends.

Following closely on the heels of this tradition is Eiler's Inn, owned and operated by Henk and Annette Wirtz. ("Henk and I came as guests of the inn in 1979 and bought it in 1981," says Annette.) Eiler's is a small establishment, despite its twelve rooms, arranged around a marvelous fountain courtyard that is definitely more Hispanic than Scandinavian. Cheese and a fruit board greet the newly arrived guest, as do complimentary champagne or sparkling cider. (Afternoon tea is also served around the courtyard fountain.) There is often live music during the wine hour on Saturdays. Both Annette and Henk are well acquainted with the area, and are happy to recommend local eating and entertainment spots.

There is a fireplace in the parlor, and a library is generously stocked with games and puzzles; there is also an attractive sun deck on the second floor. Rooms are decorated with a southern California 1940s motif (the premises began as a hotel in the early 1940s): vintage TV's, rose-patterned rugs, and speckled linoleum floors look as though they might have been part of a film set for *Chinatown* — if there had been a bed and breakfast inn as comfortable as this one in the film of that name. (All rooms have a private bath.)

The buffet-style breakfast is served in the courtyard between 8:30 and 10:30. It includes fresh fruit in a seashell, tomato or orange juice, hard-cooked eggs, pastries, and freshly ground coffee. The courtyard at Eiler's Inn is one of the most pleasant places imaginable to begin one's day, and in the bright smiles and good company of Henk and Annette one is assured that the tradition of friendliness personified by Eiler Larsen is very much alive.

The Carriage House

1322 Catalina
Laguna Beach, California 92651; (714) 494-8945

INNKEEPERS:	*Vernon, Dee, and Tom Taylor; Rik Lawrence.*
ACCOMMODATIONS:	*Six suites, all with private bath; twin, double, queen-, and king-size beds.*
RESERVATIONS:	*Three to four weeks recommended.*
MINIMUM STAY:	*Two nights on weekends through the summer.*
DEPOSIT:	*First night's lodging.*
CREDIT CARDS:	*Not accepted.*
RATES:	*Moderate to expensive.*
RESTRICTIONS:	*None.*

Southern California has its own unique style when it comes to bed and breakfast — especially when contrasted with the inns of the north coast. Perhaps the climate evokes a more casual atmosphere; perhaps it has something to do with the architectural styles of the area as well. Take The Carriage House as a case in point. Here you have six suites surrounding a central brick courtyard in a horseshoe-shaped fashion. (This arrangement is similar to Eiler's Inn, the other Laguna Beach bed and breakfast.)

Each suite features its own parlor, separate bedroom, and fully equipped kitchen. Room decors play on themes like Green Palms (forest-green walls and carpet, white woodwork, white wicker furniture, a ceiling fan, and, as one would expect — potted palms), Lilac Time (cranberry and lilac tones, French doors that open to the courtyard), Primrose Lane, Mockingbird Hill, Mandalay, and Home Sweet Home (calico and gingham).

The focal point of the inn is Grandma Bean's dining room, where guests of the inn enjoy a buffet-style breakfast from 8:30 to 10:00: hot and cold cereals, coffee cake and English muffins, fresh fruit, two different juices (orange is one), coffee, and tea.

This is a family-owned and -operated affair (Dee Taylor and husband Vernon are the resident innkeepers; son Tom and Rik Lawrence are co-owners) located on a quiet residential street just two blocks from the beach and a few more from the heart of the village.

Laguna is a town people fall in love with as well as in. Hand-holding is as popular here as jogging and cycling, and stealing a kiss as common as stealing the show — in this case the original works of art at the annual Festival of Arts and Pageant of the Masters held each year throughout July and August.

Rock Haus

410 Fifteenth Street
Del Mar, California 92104; (619) 481-3764

INNKEEPERS:	*Tom and Carol Hauser.*
ACCOMMODATIONS:	*Eight rooms, two with private bath; twin, queen-, and king-size beds.*
RESERVATIONS:	*Two to three weeks recommended.*
MINIMUM STAY:	*Two nights on weekends, Memorial Day through Labor Day.*
DEPOSIT:	*Full amount.*
CREDIT CARDS:	*MC, VISA.*
RATES:	*Moderate to expensive.*
RESTRICTIONS:	*No children. No pets.*

T he realtor who showed me this house said the original architect had a bed and breakfast in mind," Tom Hauser said jokingly as we shared a cup of coffee and some banana-nut bread on the sun porch of the Rock Haus one Thursday morning.

We were alone. All the other guests had chosen to sleep in; I had been tempted to do the same myself. What made Tom's remark so amusing was the fact that the Rock Haus was built at the turn of the century, long before bed and breakfast as we know it in this country today was established — let alone fashionable. But I could see that the notion wasn't too far afield, as the house (with its eight bedrooms and five baths) is perfect for a bed and breakfast — one of the finest on the south coast, I might add. Jacqueline Killeen, author of the best-selling *Country Inns of the Far West* would agree. She selected the Rock Haus as one of the top six new inns to open since 1977 in article recently penned for the *San Francisco Examiner*'s *California Living* section.

This California bungalow sits perched on a hill overlooking the Pacific. The quaint village of Del Mar with its outdoor cafes and shops and unspoiled beach is just two blocks below. The living room, which has been both a gambling parlor and a church sanctuary, is now filled with traditional furnishings, a player piano, a rocking horse from England (although Tom has always wanted a *racehorse*), and a brick fireplace with a backgammon board in the inglenook.

I occupied "Top o' the Rock," a very private hideaway with a cooling ocean breeze. The delicately patterned gold, green, and white wallpaper was accentuated by white woodwork; a white eyelet comforter with matching pillow shams and dust ruffle covered the queen-size bed. The love seat provided an ideal spot for cuddling and cooing. Old photographs of a young Bing Crosby at the Del Mar racetrack added a touch of interest. Another popular accommodation is the Huntsman's Room, masculine in decor with its fireplace, king-size bed, and private bath. But no matter which room you choose (Whale Watch, the Wicker Garden, Court Room, or Wren's Nest), you can't go wrong.

After breakfast (which also includes fresh fruit, cheese, orange juice, and coffee), plan to spend the day at the beach or an afternoon at the renowned Del Mar racetrack (the season runs from July to mid-September), stroll around town, or drive south to San Diego to visit the zoo, Sea World, or Balboa Park.

"I try not to take all this for granted," Tom continued as I prepared to be on my way. "Without exception people love this place — and after all, how many other professions can you think of where you get stroked every day?"

Britt House

406 Maple Street
San Diego, California 92103; (714) 234-2926

INNKEEPERS:	*Daun Martin and Charlene Browne.*
ACCOMMODATIONS:	*Nine rooms, one with private bath; double and queen-size beds.*
RESERVATIONS:	*One week for weekdays, six weeks for weekends.*
MINIMUM STAY:	*Two nights on weekends.*
DEPOSIT:	*First night's lodging.*
CREDIT CARDS:	*AE, MC, VISA.*
RATES:	*Moderate to expensive.*
RESTRICTIONS:	*Children discouraged. No pets.*

I t is not only San Diego's only bed and breakfast inn (at the time this was written), but one of the best anywhere. "From Mendocino to the stormy coast of Maine," raves the *LA Times,* "it is without a doubt the most perfectly restored Victorian serving America's travelers today." Such tributes by a large metropolitan newspaper do not come every day; and when one visits this romantic gabled and turreted Queen Anne delight, one begins to understand what the shouting is all about.

Set in a neighborhood experiencing an extensive renovation of Victorians, Britt House was built in 1887 for Eugene Britt, an attorney active in civic and state affairs. (It was later owned by the Scripps family, famous in newspaper publishing circles.) It was discovered by Daun Martin, who sank over $100,000 into restoring the proud old mansion. One of its most impressive — and justly famous — features is a stained-glass window two stories high, backing a winding staircase. Screens of wooden beads grace the doorways; hardwood floors and old wood paneling are used with the utmost imagination and taste.

The furnishings in the guest rooms enhance the romantic mood. The Windsor Room contains a queen-size bed with an ornately carved canopy draped in velvets of cerise and crimson. The Governor's Room overlooks a garden, and its blue and white color scheme is enhanced by the personal furniture of Gov. Robert Waterman, the state's seventeenth governor. The Eastlake Room is done in caramel, cream, and burgundy; one can see the ocean while sitting at its gateleg table, and its Belgian rug, carpet-backed reclining rocker, and Eastlake dresser add to the sense of luxury. Fresh fruit, homemade cookies, and candy kisses are available in all rooms, and one bath has a Finnish sauna.

Breakfast is both full and imaginative. On Sundays, for example, Daun fixes her famous dish of fresh fruit smothered in whipped cream flavored with Grand Marnier, Mexican vanilla, orange zest, and nutmeg — with a strawberry on top. The homebaked yeast bread is accompanied with sweet butter and jam. The Viennese roast coffee is prepared filter-drip style. Weekday fare also includes shirred eggs with cheese, and choice of teas.

Bed and Breakfast Referral Services

Following is a list of agencies that book reservations and refer travelers to bed and breakfast inns as well as to accommodations in private homes. These services are gaining in popularity, and the rooms in private homes include breakfast along with overnight lodging at very affordable rates (from $15 up per night).

Operations vary. Some services charge the traveler an annual membership fee, while others take their commissions from the host providing the lodging. In some cases the agencies provide lists or directories of the homes they contract with and leave the arrangements up to you.

American Family Inn/Bed & Breakfast San Francisco
(415) 931-3083
P.O. Box 349
San Francisco, CA 94101

A reservation service with homes in San Francisco, Marin County, Monterey/Carmel, the Wine Country, and the Gold Country (also some Los Angeles locations). Rates range from $40 to $85 per night; no membership fee.

Bed & Breakfast International
(415) 525-4569 or 527-8836
151 Ardmore Road
Kensington, CA 94707

A reservation service with homes in all areas of travel interest in California. Rates from $30 to $85, double occupancy; no membership fee.

New Age Travel/International Spareroom
(619) 436-9977
P.O. Box 518
Solana Beach, CA 92075

Publishes a directory of homes worldwide (many in California), providing bed and breakfast through the International Spareroom reservation service. Room rates range from $26 to $65 per night; directory cost is $4.

Rent-A-Room International
(714) 638-1406
11531 Varna Street
Garden Grove, CA 92640

Homes in southern California; $25 to $55 per night.

Home Suite Homes
(408) 733-7215
1470 Firebird Way
Sunnyvale, CA 94087

Homes in northern California; room rates $40–$90.

Bed and Breakfast West Coast
(805) 684-3524
4744 Third Street
Carpinteria, CA 93013

West Coast referrals; room rates from $30 up.

Digs West
(714) 739-1669
8191 Crowley Circle
Buena Park, CA 90621

A reservation service for California homes from Sacramento to San Diego; rates $25-plus single, $30-plus double.

Northwest Bed and Breakfast
(503) 246-8366
7707 Southwest Locust Street
Portland, OR 97223

Western states and western Canada referrals; annual membership fee $15 single, $20 double; includes directory. Room rates $18–$30 single, $24–$25 double; family rates available.

California Bed and Breakfast
No Telephone
P.O. Box 1551
Sacramento, CA 95807

A California referral service that does business by mail only. Annual membership $15; rooms $15–$30 per night.

Bed & Breakfast Exchange
(707) 963-7756
P.O. Box 88
St. Helena, CA 94574

A referral service for Napa, Sonoma, Mendocino, and Humboldt counties. Room rates start at $35 per night.

Homestay
(805) 927-4613
P.O. Box 326
Cambria, CA 93428

A reservation service for bed and breakfast lodging in private homes. Geographic coverage: "Hearst Castle Country" and the central California coast. Room rates $35–$60.

Seaview Reservations
(714) 494-8878
P.O. Box 1355
Laguna Beach, CA 92652

A bed and breakfast reservation service for private homes, mostly in and around Laguna Beach. Rates from $45 up; one-time membership fee of $5.

Megan's Friends
(805) 544-4406
1296 Galleon Way, No. 2
San Luis Obispo, CA 93401

A membership organization that provides a reservation
service; $10 annual fee. Listings include private homes
and guest houses in California, concentrating in the
central coast. Room rates from $30 up.

Eye Openers Bed & Breakfast Reservations
(818) 684-4428
P.O. Box 694
Altadena, CA 91001

A reservation service for homes in the greater Los Angeles
metropolitan area, Santa Barbara, and Palm Springs.
Rates from $30 to $60 per night; one-time membership
fee $5.

Carolyn's Bed & Breakfast Homes of San Diego
(619) 435-5009
P.O. Box 84776
San Diego, CA 92138

A reservation service for San Diego County, with several
homes located around Los Angeles (Pasadena, North
Hollywood). Rates from $20 up.

Visitor's Advisory Service
(415) 521-9366
1516 Oak Street, No. 327
Alameda, CA 94501

Short-term bed and breakfast home accommodations in
San Francisco and the Bay Area. Rates $25–$45 single,
$30–$75 double.

P.T. International
(800) 547-1463; (503) 245-0440 in Oregon
1318 Southwest Troy Street
Portland, OR 97219

A reservation service representing homes as well as inns in 48 U.S. states and abroad. Phone for rate information. No membership fee.

Bed and Breakfast of Los Angeles
(818) 889-7325/8870
32127 Harborview Lane
Westlake Village, CA 91361

A reservation service for private homes and a few small inns throughout the greater Los Angeles area — from Ventura (north) to San Juan Capistrano (south). Room rates from $18 to $60; $5 reservation fee.

Napa Valley Tourist Bureau
(707) 253-2611
P.O. Box 3240
Yountville, CA 94599

A reservation service for inns, homes, and hotels in the Napa Valley. Rates from $45 to $125; $5 reservation fee.

Bed & Breakfast in the Desert
(619) 320-1676
104 South Indian Avenue
Palm Springs, CA 92262

A Palm Springs area reservation service specializing in private homes with swimming pools, tennis courts, Jacuzzi, and golf. Rates range from $25 to $75 per night.

American Historic Homes
(714) 496-7050
P.O. Box 336
Dana Point, CA 92629

A nationwide reservation service that provides bed and breakfast in private homes of historic significance; many California locations. Room rates $25–$55, double occupancy; $3 booking fee.

Bed and Breakfast Associations

Regional associations assist the traveler with information on bed and breakfast accommodations in their geographic area by providing group brochures and central telephone referral services. The associations listed below welcome your call or letter.

Bed & Breakfast Association of Napa Valley
P.O. Box 2147
Yountville, CA 94599

Central referral number: (707) 944-1222; send $1 for brochure.

Sacramento Innkeepers' Association
2209 Capitol Avenue
Sacramento, CA 95816

(916) 441-3214; free brochure.

Mendocino Coast Innkeepers Association
P.O. Box 1141
Mendocino, CA 95460

Send $1 for group brochure.

Bed & Breakfast Innkeepers of Santa Cruz
   and Half Moon Bay
P.O. Box 464
Santa Cruz, CA 95061

An association referral service: (408) 425-1818; phone or send for free brochure.

Bed & Breakfast Inns of the Gold Country
P.O. Box 1375
Murphys, CA 95247

(209) 728-2897; send legal-size self-addressed stamped
envelope for free brochure.

Bed & Breakfast Innkeepers of the Monterey Peninsula
500 Martin Street
Monterey, CA 93940

(408) 375-8284; free brochure.

The Inns of Point Reyes
P.O. Box 145
Inverness, CA 94937

An information and referral service: (415) 663-1420;
brochure available.

Bed and Breakfast Inns of Humboldt County
P.O. Box BC-40
Ferndale, CA 95536

(707) 786-4000. Free county brochure available; $1 for a
set of individual inn brochures plus information on the
area.

Amador County Bed and Breakfast Inns
215 Court Street
Jackson, CA 95642

(209) 223-0416; send for free brochure.

Association of Bed & Breakfast Innkeepers of San Francisco
737 Buena Vista West
San Francisco, CA 94117

(415) 626-8777; brochure available for legal-size
self-addressed stamped envelope.

Bed-and-Breakfast Innkeepers of Northern California
710 Fourteenth Street
San Francisco, CA 94114

(415) 431-4770; for free brochure send legal-size
self-addressed stamped envelope.

Bed and Breakfast American Style $10.95
    by Norman T. Simpson
Berkshire Traveller Press
Stockbridge, MA

Bed & Breakfast Homes Directory — West Coast $7.95
    by Diane Knight
Knighttime Publications
P.O. Box 591
Cupertino, CA 95014

Lists private homes in California, Oregon, and
Washington.

Bed & Breakfast U.S.A. $6.95
    by Betty R. Rundback and Nancy Kramer
E.P. Dutton, Inc.
RD 2, P.O. Box 355-A
Greentown, PA 18426

Northern California Inns
    Toby Smith, Publisher
P.O. Box 3383
Santa Rosa, CA 95402

A newsletter; reviews of bed and breakfast and country
inns in northern California. $20 annually. Special reports
on bed and breakfast inns in specific areas of California
also available at $7.50 each; send for list.

The Bed 'n Breakfast Directory $4.00
P.S. Publications
P.O. Box 2512
Fairfield, CA 94533

A directory of bed and breakfast booking agencies in the U.S., Canada, Mexico, and other foreign countries.

Bed & Breakfast Almanac $4.50
B&B Productions
P.O. Box 295
St. Helena, CA 94574

A guide to accommodations and activities in the Napa Valley wine country.

Bed & Breakfast North America $10.95
   by Norma Buzan
Betsy Ross Publications
3057 Betsy Ross Drive
Bloomfield Hills, MI 48013

A directory of bed and breakfast reservation services, small inns, and individual guest houses in the U.S., Mexico, and Canada.

The Bed & Breakfast Guide
   for the U.S. and Canada $9.95
   by Phyllis Featherston and Barbara F. Ostler
The National Bed & Breakfast Association
P.O. Box 332
Norwalk, CT 06852

Lists over 400 bed and breakfast homes and family-run inns.

Hostlist $5.95
The American Bed & Breakfast Association
P.O. Box 23294
Washington, D.C. 20026

A compact guide to bed and breakfast reservation services and hosts (including inns as well as private homes) you can contact directly. U.S. coverage.

A Treasury of Bed & Breakfast $12.95
The American Bed & Breakfast Association

P.O. Box 23294
Washington, D.C. 20026

Descriptions of over 2,700 homes offering bed and
breakfast in North America.

California B&B Inns   FREE
California Office of Tourism
1121 L Street, Suite 103
Sacramento, CA 95814

A statewide listing of nearly 200 bed and breakfast inns
and host homes. For a free copy send a stamped (37¢)
self-addressed business-size envelope to above address.

Bed and Breakfast Publications

Country Inns of the Far West: California $7.95
    by Jacqueline Killeen
101 Productions
834 Mission Street
San Francisco, CA 94103

Reviews of country inns and bed and breakfast inns.

The Great American Guest House Book $7.95
    by John Thaxton
Burt Franklin & Company
235 East Forty-fourth Street
New York, NY 10017

The Complete Guide To Bed & Breakfasts,
   Inns & Guesthouses $9.95
    by Pamela Lanier
John Muir Publications
P.O. Box 613
Santa Fe, NM 87504

The California Bed & Breakfast Book $7.95
    by Kathy Strong
The East Woods Press
429 East Boulevard
Charlotte, NC 28203

Index